THE
EQUAL RIGHTS
AMENDMENT

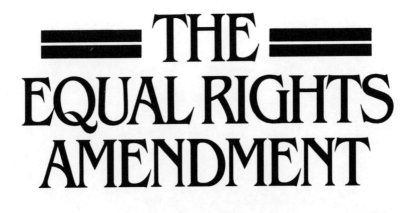

THE EQUAL RIGHTS AMENDMENT

THE HISTORY AND THE MOVEMENT

SHARON WHITNEY

FRANKLIN WATTS
New York/London/Toronto/Sydney
1984

Library of Congress Cataloging in Publication Data

Whitney, Sharon.
The equal rights amendment.

Bibliography: P.
Includes index.
Summary: Examines the ERA movement, its criticisms,
and its ultimate defeat in Congress.
1. Sex discrimination against women—Law and
legislation—United States—Juvenile literature.
2. Women—Legal status, laws, etc.—United States
—Juvenile literature.   3. Women's rights—United
States—Juvenile literature.   4. Feminism—United
States—Juvenile literature. [1. Sex Discrimination
against women—Law and legislation.   2. Women's
rights.   3. Feminism]   I. Title.
KF4758.Z9W44   1984   342.73′0878   84-11817
ISBN 0-531-04768-7   347.302878

5

CONTENTS

For Rosalie, Margaret, Jane,
and the two Dianas.
And for my mother, Helen.

THE
EQUAL RIGHTS
AMENDMENT

FROM ADAMS
TO PAUL:
150 YEARS OF
ACTIVISM

Nearly everyone today has heard of the women's movement. Since *women's liberation* was born in the late 1960s, women's efforts to achieve legal and social equality in American society have been in the public eye. The campaign to ratify the federal Equal Rights Amendment has been in the headlines, and everyone knows that the ERA went down to defeat in 1982 in spite of widespread public support. But how many people who watch television news or glance at the newspapers know that this latest struggle to secure equal rights for women is not the first of its kind? It is just the latest episode in a long-running campaign.

The women who recently rallied for the ERA in state capitals such as Tallahassee and Springfield, who rang doorbells in the small towns of Utah and North Carolina, who sat up past midnight in Oklahoma and into the night in Washington, D.C., writing leaflets, planning information campaigns, working on ways to persuade state legislators to ratify the Amendment, were not a "new breed of woman," as journalists sometimes described them. *Feminism*—activity in behalf of the political, economic, and social equality of the sexes—is as old as the country itself. "Women's rights," "equal rights," and "the Equal Rights Amendment" were all rallying cries in the nineteenth century. And even before that, there were *feminists*, although the term was not then in use.

To better understand the present women's movement and the campaign for the ERA, one should look at the history of female activism in the United States. It begins in the eighteenth century.

In the years surrounding the birth of the American republic many women worked vigorously to overthrow British rule and to create a new democracy. One way to protest the British was to hit them in the pocketbook, and the Daughters of Liberty were among the first to organize boycotts on British products. Female patriots agreed to weave their own cloth for family clothing rather than to buy imported silk and linen. "Homespun" became a symbol of righteous protest in the 1770s, just as blue jeans came to signify the protest movements of the 1970s. (The difference was that hardworking women had to make the cloth and then make the clothes, whereas protestors in the twentieth century got their jeans from the nearest shop.)

In New England, women organized Anti-Tea Leagues to object to British taxes on their favorite drink. They boycotted tea and encouraged their families to drink herbal brews and even coffee. Female protests were the background for more famous events like the Boston Tea Party.

In a small town in North Carolina a group of women published the *Edenton Proclamation*. The women said it was both their right and a duty to stand up and resist the British. They did not want to be protected from the confrontation. And when the Revolution turned into actual armed rebellion, dozens of women in different colonies disguised themselves as men in order to pick up guns and join the fight. Thousands of others went to the battlefields as nurses, doctors, cooks, laundry workers, maids, and wagon tenders.

There was in the Revolution an inner circle of leaders who came to be known as the "Founding Fathers." Among them they created the foundations of the new government, testing their ideas in public writings and private correspondence. An important correspondent in this group was one who would never be known as a "founder." Mercy Otis Warren communicated frequently with Thomas Jefferson, George Washington, John Adams, Elbridge Gerry, and others. In discussions about how the new nation should be governed, she argued in behalf of states' rights. Warren feared too much power in the federal government and wanted to see strong limits that would prevent the abuse of such power. Her essays for the public on these matters were published anonymously or under a male pen name. It wasn't respectable for a woman to express her opinions in public, but her correspondents knew her well and appreciated her opinions.

John Adams admired Mercy Warren. "God Almighty has entrusted her with powers for the good of the world which instead of being a fault to use, it would be criminal to neglect," he said. But at the same time that he appreciated the contributions Warren and other women made to political thought and to the Revolution, it did not occur to him to include women as full citizens in the new government. It was Abigail Adams, John's wife, who made a case for women.

An accomplished money manager, farmer, and businesswoman, Abigail learned these jobs by being thrust into them. It was she who maintained home and property for ten years while John was away from home building a career as a revolutionary and statesman. In John's absence, Abigail wrote hundreds of letters to him, signing them "Portia" in honor of Shakespeare's idealistic, justice-loving heroine. These letters were often about the emerging nation and the new government. In one, Abigail reminded John of the unfairness of an all-male power structure.

> By the way, in the new code of laws which I suppose it will be necessary for you to make, I desire you would *remember the ladies* and be more generous and favorable to them than your ancestors! Do not put such unlimited power in the hands of husbands. Remember all men would be tyrants if they could. If particular care and attention is not paid to the ladies, we are determined to foment a rebellion, and will not hold ourselves bound by any laws in which we have no voice or representation.

The American Revolution was a direct response to a people's being governed without their having a say in it: government without representation. Yet when Abigail Adams argued that women also deserve to decide their own affairs, John Adams treated Abigail's argument as a joke. In effect John said, In these days of revolution, everybody's getting uppity, and now it's women. But don't worry your little head about anything, Abigail. Women really run the country, anyway. If we gave you legal rights, we men would be completely at your mercy:

As to your extraordinary code of laws, I cannot but laugh!
We have been told that our struggle has loosened the bonds
of government everywhere—children and appren-
tices...schools and colleges...Indians and Negroes grew
insolent. But your letter was the first intimation that another
tribe more numerous and powerful than all the rest, were
grown discontented....Depend on it, we know better than
to repeal our masculine systems. Although they are in full
force, you know they are little more than theory. We are
obliged to go fair and softly, and you know in practice we
are the subjects. We have only the name of masters, and
rather than give up this which would completely subject us
to the despotism of the petticoat, I hope General Washington
and all our brave heroes would fight!

When in 1789 the Constitution of the United States was adopted,
Abigail Adams's urgent request to "remember the ladies" was forgotten. The document did not include women, or black men, or red
men. When the Founding Fathers reasoned that government must
have the consent of the governed, and talked about the natural equality of all human beings, they didn't mean to secure equal rights for
all persons in the new federal government system. In this regard the
great documents of American history—the Declaration of Independence, the Constitution, and the Bill of Rights—merely reflected
the prejudices of the day.

The laws that the colonists—and new Americans—lived under
were based on the criminal and civil codes of English common law.
This was a set of laws that evolved from two main ideas. In criminal
law, a person was considered innocent until proven guilty. Women
had no quarrel with this. But in civil law, the main principle was
the right of an individual male to own property. Under civil law,
women were seldom entitled to the legal safeguards that men enjoyed,
although single women could claim some of the same rights. For
instance, single women could go into business, make contracts, sue
for payment of debts, and so on. But married women were not
allowed by law to do any of these things, and were entirely dependent
on their husbands' goodwill and capabilities for support and security.

An English lawyer, William Blackstone, was the most popular
interpreter of English common law. His writings on law and marriage
were taken as gospel by many American lawyers. The "legal existence

of the woman is suspended during the marriage, or at least incorporated and consolidated into that of the husband, under whose wing, protection and cover, she performs everything," Blackstone said. This view of marriage became fixed in the American system. Two hundred years later, writer Shana Alexander compiled a *State-by-State Guide to Women's Legal Rights*. Her finding: ". . . when two people marry they become in the eyes of the law one person, and that one person is the husband!" In many states, the laws regarding marriage had stayed fixed since the days of Blackstone.

According to most American laws, all of a woman's possessions became the property of her husband in marriage. The moment the vows were spoken, a woman's land, clothing, jewelry, money—even any wages she might earn—became her husband's. A married woman could not buy or sell anything without her husband's permission. She could not sign a contract, sue, or be sued. If her husband died without leaving a will, a woman was entitled to no more than the *use* of one-third of his estate. The rest of the estate went to any male heirs, and when the woman died, so did her one-third share. It could be said that a married woman had no legal identity. She could not own her own home or control her own possessions. Legally, she did not even own her own clothes. No state granted a woman the right to vote or in any way to participate in the making of laws that affected her. In fact, she did not exist as a person in her own right. Her relationship to property made this clear.

To be fair, there were some positive features in the new American laws which didn't exist in English common law. A married woman was guaranteed the right to share her husband's home, even though she couldn't be a co-owner; she was entitled to support, even if her husband left her; and she had the right to be protected from domestic violence. But there was a kind of *Catch-22* in this. (A Catch-22 means you can have it if you can get it, but you can't get it unless you already have it.) Without being able to go to court and sue her husband, a woman could not enforce these rights. The only way a woman could sue her husband would be if the court would allow her brother or her father to bring a lawsuit in her behalf. So her safety and security still depended on the goodwill of male relatives.

For the rich, there were sometimes other options. In a few states, those born into wealthy families could keep their own property and cash through the terms of a *marriage contract*. And, through an *equitable trust* a married woman could keep whatever she was given or inherited after marriage. But such agreements were designed to keep wealth within a family line, not to give economic power to women. They had little effect on the lives of ordinary people.

It was frustration and anger about the discrimination in property laws and other conditions affecting the lives of women that finally led to the organization of the first feminist protest in the United States. Historians date the beginning of the women's rights movement back to that convention in 1848 at Seneca Falls, New York. The women credited with drawing attention to "the social, civil, and religious condition and rights of woman" were Lucretia Mott of Philadelphia and Elizabeth Cady Stanton of Seneca Falls.

Working as volunteers in the antislavery movement, Mott and Stanton discovered how it was to work hard for a political cause and still be treated as inferior citizens. In 1840 the women went to the World Anti-Slavery Convention in London. There they had a large dose of what twentieth-century feminists would call "consciousness raising"—whereby women analyze the situation they are in and become aware of their real status in life. Mott was an official delegate, yet she was not allowed to speak at the convention. All the female delegates were silenced and even made to sit out of sight behind curtains in the balcony, rather than take part in the lively discussions on the floor of the convention. Sitting behind the curtain, feeling insulted and angry over being isolated from the action, Mott and Stanton talked about other kinds of sex discrimination they had seen. The list included no free choice for women in education or job opportunities. There was no economic independence possible under state and federal property laws. With women not having the right to vote, they had no representation at any level of government. It was their opinion that women as citizens had no more real political power than children.

From the antislavery convention, Mott and Stanton returned to the United States to work for women's causes. Mott tried to raise support for women's suffrage, believing that the vote was crucial for women's progress. In New York state, Stanton helped get the Married Woman's Property Rights Act passed by the state assembly, granting married women the right to own real estate. When the two old friends finally met in Seneca Falls to plan the historic convention, they were experienced organizers. With other local women they planned a convention program and wrote up a Declaration of Sentiments. It was in part modeled after the Declaration of Independence:

We hold these truths to be self-evident: that all men *and* *women* are created equal; that they are endowed by their creator with certain inalienable rights, that among these are life, liberty, and the pursuit of happiness.

After the eloquent beginning, the Declaration parted from its model and went on to state clearly and without apology what grievances the women had against the American legal and social system.

He (man) has never permitted her (woman) to exercise her inalienable rights to the elective franchise.

He has compelled her to submit to laws in the formation of which she has no voice.

He has withheld from her the rights which are given to the most ignorant and degraded men. . . .

He has made her, if married, in the eye of the law civilly dead. . . .

He closes against her all the avenues to wealth and distinction, which he considers most honorable to himself. As a teacher of theology, medicine, or law, she is not known. . . .

He has endeavored . . . to destroy her confidence in her own powers, to lessen her self-respect, and to make her willing to lead a dependent and abject life.

The Declaration was hard-hitting, but it was approved by most of the three hundred women and men at the convention. One participant, former slave Frederick Douglass, spoke passionately in support of the clause which called for women's right to vote. Down in New York City, newspapers were fascinated with the Seneca Falls proceedings. One paper had fun lampooning the convention as a lot of nonsense; another paper took it seriously and asked Stanton to write an editorial explaining her views. Good or bad, the newspaper publicity helped carry the idea of a platform for women's rights to other states where similar conventions were then held. The first wave of organized feminism was on the move.

Elizabeth Cady Stanton became a close friend of Susan B. Anthony, "the guiding mind" of the nineteenth-century women's movement. Stanton and Anthony organized more conferences to stir public opinion. They wrote speeches, drew up petitions, and worked into the dark hours of the night together, sometimes arguing furiously over differences in their approach to issues. Stanton's seven children thought it was a wonder that the two remained friends. "After an argument they never explained to each other, nor apologized, nor wept, nor went through a make-up period, as most people do." Their commitment to women's rights was much deeper than any differences in opinion.

In 1860, thanks to the "incessant prodding and petitioning of Susan B. Anthony and her women," the New York assembly amended the Married Woman's Property Rights Act. The law now permitted a married woman to control both her own property and her wages; for the first time she became coguardian of her children; and if she were widowed she now received the same rights to her husband's property that, had she died first, he would have had to hers. This "liberating legislation" became the model for similar laws in several other states, although it had been a fight to get it passed in New York.

Opposition to women's rights was often bitter and cruel. Hostile reporters liked to describe female activists as hard and abrasive. The *New York World* wrote, "Susan B. Anthony is lean, cadaverous, and intellectual, with the proportions of a file and the voice of a hurdy-gurdy." Women of ideas were often described as ugly, repellent creatures, while women who never made waves were more likely to be called "demure," "lovely," and "feminine."

But concern for women's causes was more or less buried in the 1860s as the Civil War divided the country over the issue of slavery. Feminists—many of whom had worked for the freeing of slaves as well as for women's rights—now circulated petitions supporting the Thirteenth Amendment, which would end slavery. Anthony worked for the American Anti-Slavery Society and organized the Women's National Loyal League to urge emancipation. At the end of the war the Thirteenth Amendment, freeing the slaves, was passed, but many women were painfully disappointed with the wording of a second reconstruction amendment, the Fourteenth. This introduced into the Constitution the word *male* for the first time, giving the vote to former slaves, but stating clearly that the vote was a male privilege only. This indifference to women was all that Stanton and Anthony needed to open up the National Woman's Suffrage Association to whoever would help women get the vote. They decided to accept the support of anyone—including radical trade unionists and persons like Victoria Woodhull, a free-love advocate who spent time in jail for her unpopular views. People who believed in women's rights but didn't want to be associated with characters like Woodhull, joined the more conservative American Woman's Suffrage Association, headed by Lucy Stone.

In the coming decades, feminists continued to put their case before the people, even when they risked social ridicule. Lucy Stone became a well-known orator in an age when it was thought disgraceful for a woman to be heard in public. When Stone talked about women's rights and the vote, she could expect to be called names and even hit with rotten vegetables. But Stone and others pushed past their fears and spoke up. The wave of feminism rolled on. Susan B. Anthony published a newspaper called *The Revolution*. Its motto was, "The true republic—men, their rights and nothing more; women, their rights and nothing less."

It was in the 1870s that the name *Equal Rights Amendment* was first used. This was the name attached to the first bill introduced into Congress to give women the vote. In 1878 the bill was voted on and failed.

Reform movements grew in the last part of the nineteenth century and women worked hard on a variety of issues. The Women's Christian Temperance Union (WCTU) was organized to fight alcoholism and its devastating effects on dependent families. The WCTU was a strong force for decades. In other areas, college-educated women joined forces to press for female admissions to graduate schools and to the professions. They collected research that disproved popular myths that said that higher education ruins women's health and that working women lower the wages of working men. Some reformers lobbied for protective labor legislation for women and children, and to establish juvenile courts. Others ran settlement houses for poor immigrants. By 1900, in addition to all the volunteer labor freely given in such causes, one out of five women was also a wage earner outside the home. The first cries for equal pay and equal employment opportunity were beginning to be heard. But getting the vote was still the overriding concern.

While the federal Constitution, the highest law in the land, now insured the right to vote for must qualified men, the various states continued to create their own rules about whoever else was eligible. In the early part of the twentieth century, more than a dozen states yielded to pressure and gave women the vote. But a national movement was necessary to get women's suffrage in the country at large. To organize on a national level, strong leadership was needed. Two women, Carrie Chapman Catt and Alice Paul, came forward, each bringing different qualities and styles of leadership to the task.

Alice Paul, the founder of the National Women's Party, was a dynamic, radical feminist who had learned protest techniques from British suffragists. In 1913 Paul led eight thousand women—all dressed in white—in a march on the nation's capital to force Congress to pay attention to the need for women's suffrage. The suffrage march competed with President Woodrow Wilson's inaugural parade, and while Washington police looked away, bystanders spat on the women and men slapped them and burned them with cigar butts until the march was broken up. Later, when President Wilson showed indifference to the women's cause, Paul organized strong political opposition to Wilson. In 1917 pickets began a six-month vigil at the White House. Suffragists carried signs calling Wilson a tyrant and pointing out that while he led the country into World War I to fight for democracy, there was still no democracy for women at home. When the situation didn't change, women handcuffed themselves to the White House fence and refused to move. Many protesters, including Paul, were arrested and taken to jail. There they went on a hunger strike, which made the authorities very uncomfortable. But such tactics drew widespread attention to women's suffrage.

Carrie Chapman Catt used completely different strategies from Alice Paul. She organized extensive grass-roots support for suffrage, recognizing that changing the minds of enough people would make women's suffrage seem both possible and desirable. On the national level, she believed it was foolish to attack the men in power. She frequently visited the president and was able to persuade him to speak at a national suffrage convention. She convinced him he would be remembered in history for helping women get the vote. Between looking out the White House windows at demonstrations every day and listening to Catt's gentle persuasion, President Wilson eventually agreed to use his influence in Congress to get a women's suffrage amendment passed.

Many senators and representatives were being persuaded behind the scenes not to support women's suffrage. The suffrage movement had powerful opponents who feared the changes that female votes might bring. Among these, the "invisible enemy" was the liquor lobby, an organization that collected millions of dollars in secret contributions to campaign against suffrage. The liquor industry feared that women would vote for Prohibition, which would make it illegal to manufacture, buy, or sell alcohol. Other big business interests worked to defeat women's suffrage, assuming that a woman's vote would upset the economic status quo. Industrialists feared that women would vote to end child labor in factories, and that they would back other costly labor reforms. All in all, a great deal of money was spent fighting women's suffrage, while supporters of the cause had little money with which to promote it.

In the end it was a combination of events that tipped the scales for women's suffrage. In 1919 the Eighteenth Amendment was passed. Male voters, without the help of women, had approved Prohibition. When this happened, the liquor lobby and its stand against suffrage fell apart. At the same time, the public was recognizing the contributions made by women in World War I, and there was a broad base of support for women to get the vote. So the year after the war, Congress passed the Nineteenth Amendment—also called the "Susan B. Anthony Amendment"—by a narrow margin. (It was twice defeated in the Senate before President Wilson called a special session to pass it.) It was then ratified by the required number of states in time for women to vote in the 1920 elections.

Some feminists believed that getting the vote was the end of women's struggle for equality. But Alice Paul, who had studied law and the Constitution, believed that a battle for women's rights had been won but the war was not over. Getting the vote was only one step on the road to equal rights. There remained an overwhelming number of laws, ordinances, court decisions, and administrative rulings that discriminated against people on the basis of sex. Some universal law would have to be passed to correct all these lesser laws. Paul continued to lobby members of Congress to finish the reform that had been started with the Nineteenth Amendment. And through her efforts, the first Equal Rights Amendment aimed at correcting all the various federal, state, and local laws that discriminated on the basis of sex was introduced to Congress in 1923.

The 1923 ERA was worded this way: "Men and women shall have equal rights throughout the United States and every place to its jurisdiction." But the campaign for women's suffrage was over and there was no longer a mass movement to push for such legislation. Without being pressured, few members of Congress were concerned with another amendment related to the status of women.

In the same wording this ERA would be reintroduced in nineteen subsequent Congresses. Each time it would get just a little attention and each time it would fail to be approved and sent to the states for ratification.

=2=
STATUS OF WOMEN
IN THE
TWENTIETH CENTURY

Most young adults who read this book will have grandmothers who grew up in the early twentieth century. It may be a surprise to learn that many young women in the 1920s were considered very, very modern and "emancipated" at the time. At least that was the common idea.

In 1910, a *flapper* was any pert, headstrong woman who supported women's rights. But by the 1920s, according to *Life* magazine, *Harper's Bazaar*, and *College Humour*, a flapper was the modern woman—a wild, drinking, smoking, necking, jazz-dancing female who threw away her corsets along with any social concerns. These magazines showed endless illustrations of young women with long legs, boyish figures, and no other ambition than to play, play, play. This image became the model for young women's daydreams, and a gift from heaven for the fashion industry. (In the cosmetics industry alone, companies grew from two in 1920 to eighteen thousand in 1929.) The flapper was an exciting contrast to the sober image of the Victorian woman and the suffragist, even if the flapper was most likely to be found only in romantic fiction or on the movie screen. But what were women's lives really like apart from this popular image? And why did the need for an Equal Rights Amendment persist, if women had no cares?

The real story was that while women may have dressed like flappers and movie stars, few could afford to play, play, play. Women were now working outside the home in increasing numbers, mainly in low-paying jobs in factories and retail stores and as servants and secretaries. And they were not working for fun. The federal Bureau of Labor reported that two-thirds of the eleven million working women in the 1920s and 1930s were working to help support their families. Single women who lived at home gave most of their earnings to their parents for room and board. Married women in the labor force— mostly black or foreign-born—were helping support families who often lived below the poverty line. Women with jobs had to hold on to them, no matter how poorly they were paid. Especially in the thirties, every dollar counted.

In 1928 there had been general prosperity. For the middle and upper classes it was a boom period. Everyone was singing the hit song "Makin' Whoopee," talking about the new Hollywood star Joan Crawford, and reading Viña Delmar's best-selling novel, *Bad Girl*. Then, in October 1929, stock prices began to fall drastically. On October 24 the bottom dropped out of the market. That day was known ever after as "Black Thursday," the day of the stock market crash. A financial panic set in, then a depression, and finally the ten-year Great Depression—the deepest period of economic trouble in American history. One-fourth of the labor force lost their jobs, production was down 44 percent, banks closed, factories shut down, and many people lost their homes and farms when they could no longer meet loan payments. The only good deal was an apple; there had been a surplus crop. "Apple Annies" and "Apple Marys" sold apples on street corners to feed their families.

In the economic crisis, the myth that most women were working simply to earn "pin money" for luxuries took over. Only men were recognized as legitimate breadwinners, and twenty-six state legislatures passed laws forbidding employers to hire married women. The federal government refused to employ both a husband and wife in civil service jobs; and most schools and businesses made it a practice never to hire married women. And for black women, who had almost no economic flexibility before the Depression, the situation was especially desperate. A sixty-hour work week could yield six dollars in wages for a black maid or laundress.

There was some relief in the policies of President Franklin Roosevelt. His administration's "New Deal" called for minimum wages, and when these laws were enforced, factory and domestic workers were paid more reasonably for their labor.

Still, most industries routinely paid women less than men. More women began to look to labor unions for help in getting better pay and more humane working conditions. Women had been instrumental in organizing a large, powerful organization, the International Ladies Garment Workers Union (ILGWU) in 1900. But in the 1930s while three out of four ILGWU members were female, the head of the union and most members of the board of directors were male. It was the same in other unions.

In the White House, the poor, minority persons, and women found an advocate in Eleanor Roosevelt, wife of the president. She sought remedies for individual cases of discrimination and hardship, and supported groups whose ideas were progressive and liberal like her own. She encouraged women to go into politics to change social conditions. And she persisted in her own career as an educator, writer, and public speaker, in spite of ugly public criticism about her independent activities as First Lady. Roosevelt was the object of the same kind of abuse that was directed at early feminists and suffrage workers. Some people disliked her because she dared to speak out and take action rather than stay in her "proper" place at home.

The idea that a "woman's place is in the home" was due to be forgotten, however, with the outbreak of World War II. The war started the wheels of industry turning again; the Great Depression was over. With men leaving their jobs for military service, women were urgently needed in steel mills, munitions factories, to drive cabs, pilot aircraft, and work on skilled assembly lines. Eight million women found solid employment during the war. "Rosie the Riveter" was a popular song, celebrating women at work. Rosie was the symbol of the patriotic American female, a good-natured, capable women with her hair tied back in a bandanna and a riveting gun pressed into action on the metal flank of an airplane.

Propaganda films, designed to rally female workers into the war effort, praised the likes of Rosie. (Some of them showed homemakers as idle women with nothing better to do than to play cards and gossip, while women who worked outside the home were applauded for contributing to the industrial output.) On the job, women were better satisfied because for the first time many were earning respect for their skills *and* the same wages as their male co-workers. But the situation did not last. When the war ended, returning soldiers and sailors needed their jobs back and within a year two million women were fired. The image of Rosie the Riveter faded and women were told that heavy industry was too demanding for their delicate bodies. It was said that only men could handle the hard jobs that women had been doing all along.

After the war, people believed that most women left these jobs to become full-time homemakers again. Research shows, however, that women who were fired from well-paid jobs in industry frequently had to find other employment in unskilled factory work, service occupations, and office work. They became salesclerks, waitresses, and secretaries at greatly reduced pay. It was the same story again. Women were thought of as supplemental workers, "fur-collar wives," working to buy luxuries for a home where the man was the legitimate provider. The business world used this notion to justify low salaries for women, no matter what their skills or marital status. Single women, divorced and widowed women, women who were the major support for dependent children—all were subject to discriminatory pay.

In 1950 it was determined that women's average earnings were 65 percent of those of men. Among women in the paid labor force, married workers could expect to be employed for at least twenty-five years, and unmarried workers for forty years. But American society was ignorant of these facts. At the same time that women were standing on assembly lines and punching time clocks from nine to five, the public behaved as though women played only one real role in life. As far as magazines, television, Sunday sermons, and politics were concerned, women were not workers, professionals, students, or thinkers, but only mothers and wives. The 1950s was a decade of strong social conformity, but for women it was especially narrow. Everywhere women looked, being a successful wife and mother was pictured as endlessly romantic and rewarding. The idea of preparing for lifelong work or building a career in public service, politics, athletics, or anything else, was scarcely mentioned.

Not everyone could accept the blissful picture of a whole nation of contented wives and mothers, however. One sceptic was writer Betty Friedan. Her book describing the sentimental ideas commonly held about women in this society—and the effect these ideas had on women's lives—was called *The Feminine Mystique*. This book created such an impact on people's attitudes about women that the publication date, 1963, is often named as the start of the second wave of American feminism. It certainly influenced the attitudes of many of the women who eventually led the fight for the ERA. Therefore something should be said about both the book and the period in which it was written.

The period in which Friedan wrote *The Feminine Mystique* was one in which few women even knew that their ancestors had fought for women's rights. School books said little about women's achievements. Popular magazines, novels, movies, and television were no better. The view of what "respectable" women could do in life was very limited. Most people believed in sexual stereotypes which said that men had one set of natural capabilities and women had another, and anyone who didn't fit into the mold was in trouble. (Stereotypes are commonly held ideas about people that are based on irrelevant characteristics, such as age, sex, or physical appearance.) Women were supposed to be the "Fair Sex"—peace-loving, innocent, and modest. Men were supposed to be the "Strong Sex"—self-reliant, bold, and wise. It followed that women could not be the main actors in life. Their only proper role was to be cheerleaders urging men on to great accomplishments, while they stayed on the sidelines and watched.

Women's magazines reinforced the sexual stereotypes. Stories talked about the joys of being a perfect housewife—furnishing and maintaining a modern suburban house with all one's efforts aimed at pleasing the husband, older son, younger daughter, male dog, and female cat. A happy wife hummed while she scrubbed the floors and operated her new home appliances. If she'd been to college she was somehow supposed to be content using her education to bring up children. In this perfect domestic world, women were supposed to stay ever young, attractive, dependent, and childlike themselves. In fact, many women received "allowances" from their husbands, like children. The women's magazines never mentioned the real world of jobs and political concerns beyond the white picket fence. (Nor did the magazines support women who decided not to marry or not to have children.)

In researching *The Feminine Mystique*, Betty Friedan studied social attitudes such as those found in women's magazines. She also looked at female labor statistics and did some surveys of her own. She found that half of all adult women were working forty hours a week outside the home and that many were working another thirty hours a week in the home, trying to maintain the kind of environment that ideal families were supposed to enjoy. She also discovered something very interesting in the behavior of middle-class women. While they were reported to have everything they could want in life, there nevertheless seemed to be a deep well of unhappiness under the surface of many women's lives. While some truly enjoyed living in a home-centered world, others were showing signs of something called "housewife's syndrome." These women were suffering from "anxiety attacks" and nameless fears and depression. Large numbers of women were being given tranquilizers by their doctors to control their feelings of panic. Friedan learned that these women and many others were silently asking themselves, "Is this all there is to my life?"

Friedan believed that the trouble with women was a problem in development. She said that women who were anxious and afraid when there seemed to be nothing to fear were panicked because they actually felt themselves stifled. Friedan saw a parallel between women's feelings and the crisis that adolescents go through in becoming adults. This is called an *identity crisis*: a state of anger, confusion, and helplessness brought on by the need to change one's position in life. A young adult tries to resolve this crisis by finding meaningful work and an independent identity, and thereby growing up. The women Friedan observed had never finished the business of becoming full-fledged adults. They had never been given a chance to find meaningful work or to discover who they could be separate from being somebody's wife or somebody's mother.

Ideas in *The Feminine Mystique* helped women to start thinking about their status in life. It was beginning to be apparent that many doors were closed to women because of stereotyped notions of how men and women should behave. Women began to notice different kinds of discrimination, including discrimination by the law. Even the highest courts were keeping women in a little velvet box. For instance, in 1949 the Supreme Court had ruled that women couldn't work as bartenders (were they too delicate to pour the beer or too innocent to hear barroom talk?). In 1961 the Court ruled that a Florida law excluding women from jury duty *unless they asked for it* was constitutional (were women steered away from jury duty because they lacked the strength to make hard decisions?). Whatever the reasoning, the effect of such laws was to deny women equal employment opportunities and other experiences that many male citizens took for granted.

Such laws, along with the judges' attitudes, had been around for a long time. But what was new was the criticism these laws and legal decisions received. The country was shaking itself awake after a long period of conformity and sameness, and people's ideas of what should be tolerated was changing. Many men and women decided they weren't going to sit still and put up with unfair laws and unfair treatment anymore. And just as the first wave of feminism had been born in a period of general social reform, so was the second wave. Feminism came to life again in the remarkable decade of protest and rebellion called the sixties.

The 1960s were a time of massive support for black civil rights and for the peace and ecology movements. University students, social activists, and ordinary people who had never been politically active took to the streets to march and rally around their causes. There were *freedom rides, sit-ins, and love-ins* and a great surge of belief in the power of the people to change society. In this climate of hope, the women's movement started to grow.

President John F. Kennedy, who supported black civil rights, responded to requests that the federal government start investigating women's rights. In 1961 he announced the formation of a Commission on the Status of Women. The president said, "In every period of national emergency, women have served with distinction in widely varied capacities but thereafter have been subject to treatment as a marginal group whose skills have been inadequately utilized." And almost by accident a major federal law aimed at overcoming unfair employment practices included women.

In 1964 a civil rights bill came before Congress. Title VII of the bill called for outlawing job discrimination by private employers on the basis of "race, color, religion, or national origin." In an effort to defeat the bill, a group of conservative Southern representatives added the word "sex" to the list. They figured if women's rights were coupled with black civil rights, the bill would be such a joke it would fail. But the legislation passed and Title VII became law.

Putting Title VII into effect required the organization of the Equal Employment Opportunities Commission (EEOC). It was the Commission's job to tell employers what they had to do to comply with the law and to hear complaints from people who believed they were being discriminated against. According to EEOC guidelines, an employer could not insist that only a man or only a woman could do a particular job because of "natural" male or female abilities. For instance, employers could not refuse to hire female applicants in skilled trades such as carpentry, or to hire men in traditionally female jobs such as nursing. Also, employers could not insist on hiring only men or only women for particular jobs on the grounds that the public or the other workers wanted only men or only women in those jobs.

Title VII was a powerful tool for changing private employment practices. But the first director of the EEOC was not committed to enforcing the law in respect to women, nor did the commission take a stand on sex-based "Help Wanted" ads in the newspapers. Although it was now against the law for private employers to discriminate against women, job ads continued to read: "Help Wanted—Male" and "Help Wanted—Female," thus discouraging women from seeking new job opportunities. The situation was finally corrected only because the new women's rights organizations kept their eyes on Washington. Such groups as the National Organization for Women (NOW) were watching what the EEOC and other federal agencies were doing to enforce laws like Title VII. Because of constant pressure and publicity from groups like NOW, the EEOC began to do its job more forcefully. The commission began to look seriously at sex-discrimination complaints, EEOC guidelines were given to private industry, and sex-segregated job ads in newspapers were declared illegal.

In addition to Title VII, other measures were designed specifically to help women. Executive orders issued by the president's office in 1965 and 1967 forbade sex discrimination by the federal government or by organizations doing business with the federal government. One order demanded that organizations with federal business contracts take *affirmative action* to end sex discrimination. (In other words, businesses couldn't sit back and wait for the chance to be fair. They had to make a real effort to recruit and train women to fill a certain number of jobs.)

Between Title VII and the orders for affirmative action, it was believed that the 1960s would be a breakthrough for women in getting access to more jobs and equal pay. But new laws and regulations were not enough. Private industry needed encouragement and enforcement to comply—the carrot and the stick. The government also needed some of the same treatment.

Not just EEOC, but many government agencies had the opportunity to improve the status of working women. There were countless women in government stuck at low-grade jobs, and there were thousands of government contracts for goods and services with private industry. While there were employers in both government and private industry who went along with affirmative action programs, there were many more who had no interest at all in women's rights. And since women's rights were not a priority in the various departments of the federal government, agencies made only modest efforts to educate themselves and the public in the meaning of the laws.

But while the machinery of government was barely moving to facilitate changes for women, women themselves were going into action. August 26, 1970, was the fiftieth anniversary of women's suffrage in the United States. On college campuses and in towns and cities throughout the country, thousands of women went on strike to honor early feminists and to protest the inequality of American society fifty years after that first major victory. Women who were used to working for other civil rights causes now took to the streets to make a statement about themselves. They demanded public support for child care, the right to choose abortions, and the right to pursue equal opportunities in education and in employment. They demanded whatever was needed in order to explore their own capabilities and to become more fully developed persons.

The sixties had been a catalyst. The seventies was going to be a decade of enormous growth and change. For women it would swell and burst with a whole universe of new ideas and actions. Many women would come to see themselves differently and to believe that they were entitled to much more than their mothers had ever dreamed of. In the seventies, the campaign for the ERA was inevitable.

THE SEVENTIES
AND THE
NEW FEMINISM

In the 1970s the United States witnessed a great surge of political activity within the female population. Women who belonged to seasoned groups like the American Association of University Women (AAUW), along with members of new groups such as NOW, committed themselves to finding out the true picture of women and legal equality. Meetings, seminars, and conferences were held on small college campuses and in big urban centers on subjects of interest first and foremost to women. Violence against women, female access to credit, women's place in religious institutions, women's absence in the military—it seemed that the topics would never run out.

For some groups, the most important issue was women's control over their own bodies. The right to *reproductive freedom*—deciding when and whether to bear children—was the sole focus of many groups who wanted to get rid of state laws against abortion and against dispensing birth control information. For other groups, economics was the major problem. They wanted equal pay, equal opportunity for jobs, and job flexibility for working mothers. In order to create change, women found they had to research the problems, gather evidence, and try to educate the public and public officials on the need for change. Many women believed that if you just showed people what was wrong and what was fair, unfair situations would be corrected.

The AAUW studied discriminatory laws and found that they were almost always written on the basis of stereotyped ideas about women. The laws assumed that women were passive by nature, that they were physically frail, and that they lacked the ability to reason. With this point of view, it was no wonder that lawmakers treated women as a separate class of citizen.

Women came to realize that they were part of a double standard in society. They found that men and women were being measured differently, with men adjusting the scales. Author Virginia Woolf had written that men see women from "that deep-seated desire, not so much that *she* shall be inferior, as that *he* shall be superior." Such insights became part of a growing body of feminist theory—principles that showed how females had been influenced and molded by the attitudes of a male-dominated society. In the process of putting together women's history and feminist theory, some feminists lost patience and decided that a radical transformation of society was the only answer to the problem.

Radical feminists (as they were called) wanted more than just to be heard and to lobby peacefully for social change. They wanted to completely overturn the political system in which men control all kinds of power including government, education, industry, the arts, and science. Radical feminists refused to be quiet about the unfairness of the American system. They took seriously what Susan B. Anthony said in 1868: "There shall never be another season of silence until women have the same rights men have on this green earth." They created a voice for themselves in a network of newspapers and newsletters. The publications were called *Everywhere*, *It Ain't Me Babe*, *Ain't I a Woman?*, *Off Our Backs*, *A Journal of Liberation*, and *Up from Under*.

Radical feminists wanted "Liberation, Now!" The movement for radical social reform was called women's liberation. The popular press began to pay some attention to it, although it did not distinguish between radical and more moderate members of the women's movement. "Women's libber" was a cute name given to anyone who supported women's rights. The name tended to make a joke out of serious efforts. There was generally a lot of confusion in society about what women wanted. An example could be seen in an article in the *Miami Herald* called "50 Ways Men Can Start Helping Women." The article cautioned, "Let a woman take the initiative in dating and sex if she wants to . . . and don't joke about Women's Liberation— it is a serious thing."

Ordinary women who spoke up for the first time about women's place in society were frequently called "radical." This was because most people didn't have a yardstick to know how far feminist political thought was going. Radicals were at the forefront of change, not in the mainstream. Such a leader was Kate Millet, a sculptor and the author of *Sexual Politics* (1970).

In her book, Millett defined politics as "power-structured relationships" in which one group governs another. She said that in a society dominated by men, the most important institution to get rid of is the family. The family is the principal unit for brainwashing. The idea that male power is correct and natural comes from seeing men at the head of households with other members of the family relying on their economic and social status. Furthermore, gender roles are enforced inside the family, Millett said. This is where girls learn to be passive and domestic like their mothers and boys learn to be aggressive and outer-directed like their fathers. She argued for new relationship patterns and the blending of separate male and female ways of life.

Like *The Feminine Mystique* in the sixties, *Sexual Politics* stimulated a lot of new dialogue among women in the seventies. But the chief vehicle for women's liberation were "consciousness raising" (CR) groups. These were small, weekly gatherings of women in communities across the country who met to talk about personal experiences in a male-dominated world. In these groups, women began to see that "the personal is political" in the sense that what goes on within relationships is but an extension of the ideas of personal power which individuals hold no matter where they are.

Sharing their lives in CR groups, women began to experience a sense of sisterhood, realizing they had much in common. The emotions they shared were frequently frustration and anger. Their complaints were sometimes about little things, but they discovered that little things showed how most women were playing servantlike and secondary roles.

In 1972 Jane O'Reilly wrote about "The Housewife's Moment of Truth" for *Ms.* magazine. She said that women were angry because "we have suddenly and shockingly perceived the basic disorder in what has been believed to be the natural order of things." O'Reilly called her moments of truth "clicks." This was when she put two and two together and realized there was nothing natural—or fair— about one person being used and abused by the whole household. For instance:

I watched the men in my household ignore the basket of laundry my loving hands had collected, sorted, washed and folded, and finally placed right on the couch by the television set. The family moved it to one side of the couch so they could sit down. I left it there. I put more on the couch. They piled it up. They began to dress off the couch. I began to avoid the television room. At last, guilty and crazy, my nerve failed and I carried the laundry upstairs. No one noticed. *Click.*

Along with housewives, working women were having new moments of awareness. Ruth J. Abram, executive director of Women's Action Alliance, wrote to *Ms.*:

Today, I sat in a meeting of the board of an organization of which I am a trustee. All other trustees are male. As they adjourned to hold the second part of the meeting at a club that discriminates against women, I reminded them that I was not going to join them because its membership policies were repugnant to me. While they agreed to hold no future meetings in this club, not a single man said, 'For today, why don't we just order sandwiches in.' Instead, they all walked off to the club. *Click.*

In the 1970s several feminist concepts came into popular usage. *Sexism* was a term analogous to *racism*. It described a set of deeply felt, but often unconscious, beliefs that decided people's worth on the basis of their sex and sexual roles. Feminist scholars claimed that sexist beliefs have been the basis of the whole religious, economic, and social system which keeps women down. While this concept may have been too sweeping for some people to grasp, nearly everyone could get a handle on the idea of *male chauvinism*. This term described the belief that males are born with superior capabilities in all the important areas of human activity and that females are created solely to serve males and to provide sexual pleasure. Men who defended such ideas were called "male chauvinist pigs." "MCP" became a well-known epithet.

Men like Hugh Hefner, the publisher of *Playboy* magazine, which features idealized photographs of nude women, were attacked by radical feminists as MCPs. A memo that Hefner wrote to his staff about his female critics was uncovered. It showed the hostility that was building in a war between revolutionary women and openly sexist men. Hefner told his magazine staff, "These chicks are our natural enemy.... It is time to do battle with them ... what I want is a devastating piece that takes the militant feminists apart. [They are] unalterably opposed to the romantic boy-girl society that *Playboy* promotes...."

In New York City, the Playboy Club was picketed by women. But the situation was confusing. While some feminists were embarrassed and angry that other women had to dress up as rabbits wearing high-heeled shoes and rib-crunching corsets in order to wait tables at a night club, there was also the fact that a Playboy "bunny" could make more in tips than could a salaried clerk in a nine-to-five job. Was it fair for women to attack other women who were making reasonable money even though it was in a sexist situation? With limited economic opportunities, who should say what women should do?

The fact was that women weren't doing very well as wage earners. New data on women in the labor force in the early 1970s showed that women earned fifty-eight cents to every dollar that men earned. *Time* magazine published some income statistics in an article asking, "Who's Come a Long Way, Baby?" The article noted that 42 percent of all women aged sixteen and older worked outside the home.

> Yet there is only one economic indicator in which women consistently lead men, and that is the number living in poverty. In 1968, the median salary for full-time year-round workers was $7,870 for white males, $5,314 for nonwhite men, $4,580 for white women and $3,487 for nonwhite women. On the average, a woman needs a college degree to earn more than a man does with an eighth-grade education.

In a job survey, the United States Census Bureau found that of the 441 occupations listed in the census, most women were in the 20 lowest-paid classifications. (Among these, black women were the most poorly paid. More than a quarter of all black working women were domestic workers; in 1970 their median income was $1,700.) For many women, legislation like Title VII of the Civil Rights Act of 1964 and executive orders requiring an end to discrimination just weren't doing the job. Something more was needed to jolt the system. Not only were women failing to get equal access to the job market, but the Supreme Court had also shown it wasn't going to blaze any trails to rout out sexual discrimination unless there was a political mandate to do so. That mandate was the Equal Rights Amendment, which had been languishing in Congress since 1923.

The modern campaign for the ERA began in 1967 when Alice Paul, then eighty-two, persuaded NOW to endorse the Amendment. By 1972, partly due to momentum from the civil rights movement but also because of political maneuvering by representatives such as Congresswoman Martha Griffiths, the ERA was passed by Congress.

The proposed law was simple: *Equality of rights under the law shall not be denied or abridged by the United States or by any state on account of sex.* Thirty-eight states were required to ratify the Amendment before March 1979. Within one year, thirty state legislatures gave it their stamp of approval. Leaders within the women's movement felt confident. No one saw the trouble that lay ahead.

In the mid-seventies there also arose a counter movement, opposed to many of the causes the women's movement promoted. A drive against the ERA was launched in southern and rural states, with conservative Republican Phyllis Schlafly at the helm. In one state after another, the ERA was blocked by a well-organized and well-financed opposition. As the seventies marched on, passing the Amendment began to seem questionable. But at the same time there was no doubt that women were beginning to be noticed by government. For example, women were being asked to define for themselves what they wanted.

In 1977 an International Women's Year (IWY) conference was held in Houston, Texas. It was the single biggest event of the decade for the women's movement, an event that changed many women's ideas of themselves and their capabilities. IWY was unique and powerful. It was like a "rite of passage"—a ceremony signifying that women were coming of age in their quest for a share of the nation's political power. The meeting was as historic as the convention in Senca Falls in 1848 (the first women's rights convention in America), but magnified a thousand times.

The convention was called by Congress and the administration of President Jimmy Carter. Congress provided five million dollars to plan, organize, and stage the event including preliminary conferences at the state level. The purpose of IWY was to "identify barriers that prevent women from participating fully and equally in all aspects of national life" and to recommend ways to eliminate such barriers. In November 1977, two thousand official delegates from fifty-six states and territories went to Houston to decide what legislation would best meet those ends. Along with the official delegates, there were also some twelve thousand alternate delegates and observers.

The idea was to come up with a unified National Plan of Action, although it was not expected that two thousand diverse individuals could readily agree on common goals. The delegates represented all income brackets, occupations, ages, races, and religious and political affiliations. Hispanics were represented, as well as blacks, Asian-Americans, and native Americans. There were women with advanced university degrees and women who hadn't gone past the sixth grade. Half the women who went to Houston for IWY had never been to a political convention before.

Three controversial issues quickly stood out: legal abortion, lesbian rights, and the Equal Rights Amendment. All three sparked debate—much of it emotional. Some 20 percent of the delegates were "pro-family" conservatives who feared legislation that would support any of these issues. Most conservatives saw abortion, gay rights, and the ERA as features of the same godless monster that threatened to destroy the security of the American home. Their campaign lumped the issues together. One sign that summed up the opposition said: *Woman's Libbers, E.R.A. Lesbians REPENT Read the Bible while Your* [sic] *Able*. Anti-ERA squads urged their delegates to vote against *any* resolution or recommendation that was written with neutral gender words like "spouse" or "person" instead of "man" or "wife" because neutral words were a tip-off that the resolution had been drafted by feminists.

But in spite of being well organized, the conservatives could not make a big enough dent in support for the controversial issues to defeat them. Besides dealing with voting blocs created by the National Organization for Women and other liberal groups, they had to abide by convention rules that hurt minority positions. For instance, rules said that debate on an issue could be shut off at any time by a simple majority vote of the delegates on the floor. This tactic was used to squelch conservative testimony until the convention chair, Bella Abzug, stepped in and made sure conservative leaders were heard.

Pro-abortion and pro-life delegates became angry over the sensitive issues. Both sides felt that they represented the only true moral position; few people changed their minds listening to the passionate debate. It was not surprising when the liberal majority won and legal abortion, along with a recommendation for federal and state funding to help pay for poor women's abortions, became part of the IWY National Plan of Action.

The conservatives were also up against some political "horse trading" that preceded the convention. Lesbian rights was one issue that benefited from horse trading. Before they ever got to Houston, Hispanic representatives from thirty states agreed to support a resolution calling for an end to job, housing, child custody, and credit discrimination against lesbians. The trade-off was support from the National Gay Task Force for farm worker rights and bilingual education that would benefit Hispanics.

The ERA was also strongly endorsed by all but the conservative minority, so the big three issues made it into the IWY legislative plan. Other points the convention endorsed were the creation of national health insurance; the extension of Social Security benefits for housewives; a federal campaign to educate women on their right to credit and bank loans; government-funded programs for victims of child abuse; government-sponsored rape prevention education; state-supported shelters for battered women; and a federally funded program addressing the problems of poverty, isolation, and the underemployment of rural women.

When the convention was over, it remained for officers to work out the language of proposed legislation and to send the resolutions to Congress and the president. But for the thousands of women who went to Houston, the next move was to go back home and get active in grass-roots politics. For the first time many women were feeling some sense of power and optimism gained from working with other women toward common goals. Many believed for the first time that women could become a force to be reckoned with. As one woman put it, "We are going to say to our elected officials that unless you listen to our demands we are going to get you out of office."

IWY was a big boost for feminist morale. And because the convention received a fair amount of press coverage, it also helped educate the public on women's issues including the ERA. In 1978, public opinion polls showed that a clear majority of Americans of both sexes favored passage of the Amendment. But time was running out and public opinion was not budging the recalcitrant state legislatures. The only immediate solution was to seek an extension of the March 1979 deadline. Congressional Representative Elizabeth Holtzman of New York sponsored a resolution asking for seven more years. But the House and Senate agreed to thirty-nine months, instead, making the new ratification deadline June 30, 1982.

Opponents of the ERA had seen to it that the deadline was none too generous. The Moral Majority, the Eagle Forum, and members of the Mormon Church had lobbied against the extension. These groups also wanted Congress to pass a law allowing states to rescind their earlier ratifications. When Congress said no, and states had to stand by their earlier votes, the conservative groups focused back on the state capitols. There they increased their efforts to keep any more state legislatures from endorsing the ERA. ERA supporters were put on notice that even with the thirty-nine-month extension, it wasn't going to be easy to get the necessary states' approval.

At the close of the IWY convention in 1977, journalist and ERA fund-raiser Liz Carpenter had quipped, "If I die, don't send flowers, just send three more states." At the end of the decade she could have said the same thing. Three more states were still needed for ratification.

Many women were incredulous that so many changes had taken place in the 1970s without the ERA having been approved. It seemed to some like an oversight—a mistake that would be cleared up. But others remembered history. It had taken from 1848 to 1920 for women to get the vote. It was painful, but not surprising, that the ERA had not been ratified. Legislatures that refused to budge were caught in the grip of social and political forces much older and more powerful than volunteer groups of women working for the ERA.

But at the same time that they worried, ERA supporters had no intention of merely twiddling their thumbs and hoping the required number of states would tumble their way. Voter education was something women had some experience with, so getting out information on the ERA became a priority now. In an effort to dispel some of the myths about the ERA, organizations began to publish pamphlets and workbooks showing how the Amendment would work. It was becoming clear that not many citizens knew much about the ERA. Opponents claimed it would hurt women, not help, and even ERA supporters were often fuzzy about just what the concrete effects would be. What everyone needed were the facts, supporters said, so the end of the seventies was the beginning of an overdue public information campaign.

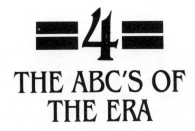

THE ABC'S OF
THE ERA

In the middle of the 1970s a public opinion poll found that women were basically uninformed about the ERA. Even though this legislation could vitally affect them, the survey showed that only a slight majority of American women—only 53 percent—even knew what it was. Three-quarters of the women polled said they didn't know enough about it to have an opinion one way or the other. One-quarter of the women who knew what the ERA was didn't know whether their home state had ratified it; and no group of women could give details about what the specific effects of the ERA would be.

It remained for various educational organizations to spell out the ABCs of the ERA. From the League of Women Voters to the American Jewish Congress, women sat down and dug into the legislative history of the Amendment, questioning lawyers and scholars in an effort to discover what the facts on the ERA might be. These are some of their findings.

THE AMENDMENT

The basic meaning of the Equal Rights Amendment is that sex cannot be a factor in determining the legal rights of anyone. The idea behind the ERA is not that women and men are exactly the same, but that *the law cannot be permitted to treat them differently solely because of their gender.*

The full text of the ERA introduced to Congress in 1971 is this:

Resolved by the Senate and the House of Representatives of the United States of America in Congress assembled (two-thirds of each House concurring therein), that the following article is proposed as an amendment to the Constitution of the United States, which shall be valid to all intents and purposes as part of the Constitution when ratified by the legislatures of three-fourths of the several States within seven years from the date of its submission by the Congress:

Section 1. Equality of rights under the law shall not be denied or abridged by the United States or by any State on account of sex.

Section 2. The Congress shall have the power to enforce, by appropriate legislation, the provisions of this article.

Section 3. This amendment shall take effect two years after the date of ratification.

THE SCOPE OF THE LAW

First of all, the ERA would take precedence over any other federal, state, or local law. It would provide an overriding mandate for equal treatment. Domestic relations law, including rules for marriage, divorce, and child custody would be affected. So would government employment practices and benefits; public education programs from kindergarten to college; job training programs sponsored by the government; labor laws; criminal justice codes; Social Security law; government pension plans; and workers' compensation practices.

The federal ERA would be the final word on sex discrimination in these areas. While laws providing such rights as equal employment opportunities for women could be made at the local and state level, they could also be reversed by the next set of lawmakers who didn't want them. With the ERA, equal treatment would be assured in spite of how political winds are blowing.

At the same time, the scope of the ERA was not unlimited. *The ERA would not apply to practices outside government jurisdiction.* In the case of privately owned industry, the 1964 Civil Rights Act was established to protect female and minority rights. The ERA would not apply there. And in the case of private lives, the ERA would have no business.

The Amendment has nothing to do with personal relationships, private actions, or social customs. These are not its focus. It is only laws that are based on assumed traits of human nature—physical, psychological, and cultural—that would be in trouble. The National Women's Division of the American Jewish Congress (AJC) tried to clear up this confusion in a booklet on the ERA.

> For example, a state junior college could not bar female students from enrolling in an auto repair course. A mother could not automatically be preferred over a father in deciding child custody. Nor could a state mete out one punishment to men and another to women for the same crime. In some states, for example, "unwritten law" is permitted as a defense to the wronged husband of an unfaithful wife—but not to the wronged wife; in another, a woman can be jailed for three years for habitual drunkeness and a man can be jailed for 30 days for the same offense. Such legally sanctioned discrimination would be invalid.

The AJC also found that a certain category of laws would be untouched by the ERA. These laws have to do with physical characteristics found in only one sex. According to the AJC, laws establishing medical leave from work for women for child*bearing* would still hold under the ERA (while work leave for child *rearing* would have to apply to both sexes). Furthermore, laws punishing male rapists would stay in effect, as would laws relating to the determination of fatherhood.

LEGISLATIVE HISTORY AND THE INTERPRETATION OF THE ERA

Final interpretation of the ERA would be up to the courts. And the way that judges spell out the meaning in respect to the ERA, or any other law, is by looking at legal precedents and studying what the lawmakers intended. Because of this, the testimony given in Congress on the ERA is of great interest. It reflects the social values that influenced Congress to approve the measure. It tells what the legislators and the public believed. Committee and subcommittee hearings, along with debate on the floors of the House and Senate, are part of the "legislative history" of the ERA, and as such would be a legal guide.

In the case of the ERA, hearings were most comprehensive in the Senate. The senators wanted to know how the ERA would affect laws relating to families, employment, military service, and criminal justice. Senators listened to testimony which filled more than a thousand pages. Lawyers, labor leaders, representatives of religious groups, and members of a wide range of women's groups gave their opinions.

People speaking against the Amendment warned the senators that they were considering a dangerous measure. Conservative Roman Catholic Church members testified that the ERA would upset God's plan. They feared it would shatter family life, which depends on woman's role in the home, maintaining the spirit and substance of the family system. They said it would destroy laws which protect women as dependent persons; some said the ERA would even destroy women's dignity.

Representatives from industry expressed their concerns about women in the workplace. If the ERA were passed, it would cause the repeal of protective labor laws, according to Mortimer Furay, an official with the Detroit AFL-CIO Council. Such laws regulate the hours women work, what kind of loads they may lift, and so forth. Furay sounded like "a gentleman of the old school." "It must be manifestly clear that women are different from men—*vive la différence*—that they are subject to inequality as a result of their sex, and it is cruel and unjustified. You must not add to it by repealing enacted law. . . ."

But some legislators didn't think that protective labor laws were really so protective. In the House hearings on the Amendment, Representative Martha Griffiths took up the protective labor law issue. She explained that laws regulating how much weight female workers could lift didn't even apply to most stores and hospitals where women worked. She also pointed out that a 1910 law, still in effect, barred women from jobs as night clerks in hotels but it didn't prevent them from scrubbing hotel floors all night at much lower wages.

Others testified that protective laws were really used to keep women from competing with men for better pay. In the interest of "protection," there were laws limiting the amount of overtime pay a woman could receive, as well as laws limiting the kind of work she could do to qualify for overtime.

Senator Marlow Cook argued that the ERA would help correct economic discrimination by giving women better job opportunities and by making equal qualifications count. The father of three daughters, Cook asked why a young woman can graduate from Harvard with a straight-"A" record and be employed at six thousand dollars a year, while a young man who graduates with a "B" average from the same college gets a job earning eleven thousand dollars?

Besides such personal testimony, written evidence was introduced into the proceedings. The most significant was a report from the 1971 *Yale Law Review* entitled "The Equal Rights Amendment: A Constitutional Basis for Equal Rights for Women." The report was written by a Yale Law School professor and three students, and was a well-researched analysis of the likely effects of the ERA on existing laws.

Concerning labor laws, the Yale report said that any legislation that gives benefits to women would have to give them to men, too. And laws that prevented women from doing specific kinds of work would probably be invalid. For example, in seven states where there are minimum wage laws for women only, men would also be entitled to a minimum wage; and in states where laws forbid women from working night jobs, those laws would be struck down.

One touchy subject that the Yale report tackled was military service. The report said the Army and Navy would have to stop looking at women as incapable of being useful. It said the ERA would require the military to "see women as it sees men—as a diverse group of individuals, married and unmarried, with and without children, possessing or desiring to acquire many different skills, and performing many varied kinds of jobs." The ERA would insist that women be allowed to enter and participate in military service on the same basis as men.

But few people were accustomed to looking at women as a human resource in the same way they viewed men. The possibility of women on the combat field was a constant hot item in the ERA debate. In spite of the Yale opinion that women would get equal consideration by the military, Senator Birch Bayh doubted women would be considered for combat service. According to Bayh:

Less than one percent of the eligible males in the whole country were ever assigned to a combat unit. It might be fair to say that this is about the same risk women would be subjected to . . . except it would be fairer to assume that the sex-neutral standards that would be established in the Armed Forces on the basis of physical competence would exclude an even greater percentage of women because of the ordinary physical standards required. . . . Just as 85 percent of those who are now in the armed services and who are men are not assigned to combat duties, so the commander would not need to send a woman into the front trenches if he felt that it would not be in the best interest of the combat unit to make such an assignment.

Former Representative Louise Day Hicks also put down the idea of women in combat service. "It is an absurd scare tactic to summon up images of girls slogging through rice paddies with M-16s and full 60 pound packs strapped on their backs," she said.

Nevertheless, it was evident that women would be drafted if a draft were called, and this picture was alarming. Opponents of the ERA told Congress that the worst *was* bound to happen. The Amendment would force mothers out of their homes and into the army, they said.

In response, it was pointed out that women might be drafted but not mothers. Women would get the same exemptions that men were used to getting when a draft was in effect; this meant that individuals with dependent children and other special responsibilities, such as holding public office, would not have to join the service.

Other emotionally charged issues were raised in the hearings. Homosexuality was one. Somehow the idea of sexual equality under the law was taken to mean the end of separate identities for males and females and a rise in homosexual life-styles. It was said the ERA would legalize homosexual marriages. Senator Bayh pointed out that the ERA refers to discrimination on the basis of gender, not sexual behavior. Simply put, what is permitted to members of one sex must be permitted to members of the other. He said the ERA:

> . . . would not prohibit a state from saying that the institution
> of marriage would be prohibited to men partners. It would
> not prohibit a state from saying the institution of marriage

would be prohibited to two women partners. All it says is that if a state legislature makes a judgment that it is wrong for a man to marry a man, then it must say it is wrong for a woman to marry a woman.

There was also the idea that the ERA would mean loss of privacy for men and women in such places as public rest rooms, school dormitories, and gymnasiums. Opponents believed there would be no more separate bathrooms if the Amendment was approved. Standards of decency were at stake, opponents said, forgetting all the "unisex" bathrooms that already existed on airplanes and in private homes. The final Senate report stated that "the Amendment would not require dormitories or bathrooms be shared by men and women." It made clear that social standards would continue to be honored.

Debate on these and other issues took place chiefly in the Senate. The ERA had been introduced and approved quickly by the House of Representatives in a vote of 354 to 23 in October 1971. Following Senate debate, it was overwhelmingly approved there, too. The Senate voted 84 to 8 in favor of the Amendment in March 1972. (A two-thirds vote of each house had been required.)

RATIFICATION

Ratification procedures are spelled out in Article V of the Constitution of the United States. Any constitutional amendment has to be approved by three-fourths of all state legislatures (thirty-eight), or by special conventions in three-fourths of the states. The ERA set out on the most common route: ratification by the legislatures.

While the Constitution does not require a time limit on the ratification process, Congress decided to impose one in the case of the ERA. Hence the seven-year deadline, later extended by thirty-nine months.

IMPLEMENTING THE LAW

How would the ERA be put into practice if it were ratified? Legal experts agreed that all laws that discriminated on the basis of sex would not be suddenly and magically rewritten the day the thirty-eighth state ratified the Amendment. Instead, it would be up to the states to start making changes.

In 1976, when thirty-four states had ratified the Amendment and passage seemed fairly certain, Susan Deller Ross, director of the American Civil Liberties Union's Women's Rights Project, told the National Press Club in Washington what she believed would happen. First of all, legislatures would have two years in which to examine and rewrite their laws; this would be done in the context of ordinary legislative business. Ross was confident that no legislature would do anything bizarre or radical in rewriting laws. For an example, she pointed to family law:

> Do you know of a single state legislature in the country likely to pass a law saying husbands don't have to support wives, or that wives have to contribute 50 percent of their money to their households, or that senior women will lose their right to be provided with a home?...By rewriting laws in terms of function instead of sex, they can pass a wide variety of politically acceptable ones which both conform to the ERA and provide protection to dependent women.

CASE STUDIES ON THE
IMPACT OF THE ERA

As the ERA was ratified by various states, government task forces were appointed to study how the Amendment would affect state laws. And at the same time, women's organizations such as the American Association of University Women (AAUW) and the League of Women Voters (LWV) studied specific issues such as credit, employment, education, family law, insurance, and Social Security to see what the ERA would do to existing regulations. A summary of these issues and how ERA would affect present laws and regulations follows.

Credit is closely related to the standard of living most people enjoy. Few people can pay cash for major items such as a house, a car, or a college education; they have to rely on loans or cerdit cards. But because their average income is lower than men's, women were not treated as good loan risks even with a steady income. This situation changed somewhat in 1974 with the federal Equal Credit Opportunity Act, which demands that institutions give credit to all worthy customers "without regard to sex or marital status." But the law was not widely understood.

Eileen Shanahan, a former *New York Times* economics reporter, had to quote from stories she herself had written about the law in order to get a credit card in her own name. "If I had trouble, the ordinary woman who wasn't as positive about the law would have lost the argument," she said. Passing the ERA would help reinforce the law, but it is not known whether the ERA would directly affect credit practices. A test case would be needed for the courts to decide whether government regulation of the banking industry is reason enough to apply the ERA to individual financial institutions.

Employment statistics have always shown impressive differences between male and female incomes. In 1956, women who worked full time earned approximately 63 percent of what men earned. In 1973, women's incomes stood at 57 percent. In 1980, the figure stood at 59 percent.

Unfair employment practices were supposed to have been corrected by the equal pay and equal opportunity laws passed by Congress in the early 1960s. If these laws had been enforced, employment statistics would read differently. The Equal Pay Act of 1963, Title VII of the Civil Rights Act of 1964, and Executive Orders 11246 and 11375 of 1968 were designed to bring equality to the workplace.

The Equal Pay Act of 1963 prohibits employers from paying men more than women (or vice versa) for jobs that require equal skill, effort, and responsibility, and that are performed under similar working conditions. The Department of Labor was charged with enforcing the law.

Title VII of the Civil Rights Act of 1964 bans discrimination based on sex, race, color, religion, and national origin. It applies to any private business that has at least fifteen employees and engages in interstate commerce. This is administered by the Equal Employment Opportunity Commission.

Executive Orders 11246 and 11375 of 1968 (issued by President Lyndon B. Johnson) outlaw discrimination in awarding government contracts over ten thousand dollars in value. The Department of Labor was supposed to see these orders carried out.

In 1975, the U.S. Commission on Civil Rights (a government agency) investigated government efforts to see that these laws were carried out. It concluded that while the laws had made many changes possible, little had been done. Efforts were found to be "fundamentally inadequate." The commision said much of the problem lay within the government itself. In particular, the Department of Labor had been indifferent. There was no consistent effort to educate employers on their responsibilities or employees on their rights. There was no push to investigate complaints or to draw up a list of penalties that would give the law clout. In short, it seemed that following through on such laws was a low priority for the government.

How would the ERA improve such a situation? It would not expand the protection offered by such laws, but it is believed it would help press the agencies into action. It would put pressure on government administrators to have a clear-cut program of law enforcement. And with penalties in view, most employers would be less likely to sidestep the law. More citizens would also be aware of their right to challenge unfair practices with the ERA.

Besides supporting the civil rights laws, the ERA would correct the federal employment and benefit systems. Women would get the same benefits as men in the workers' compensation system. Medical benefits for male and female government employees would have to be equal, as would their pension and retirement plans.

Education would be affected by the ERA. Not only public schools, colleges, and other institutions that receive government funds, but also job training programs would have to provide equal pay and equal opportunities.

In 1973, average wages for men and women who graduated from job training programs sponsored by the Department of Labor were $3.05 per hour for men and $2.36 per hour for women. The reason behind this difference was that most women were being trained in traditional, low-paid "women's jobs" such as clerical work, sales, practical nursing, and cosmetology. Few were being trained in crafts and skilled trades—higher paying occupations.

On the other side of the fence from students, female teachers also held the lowest paid jobs. Most elementary school teachers—the most modestly paid teachers—were women, while 84 percent of all public school administrators and principals—the highest paid educators—were men. In colleges and universities, where the highest rank is full professor, only 9.5 percent of these well-paid jobs were held by women.

A federal law, aimed at ending discrimination in the field of education, was passed by Congress in 1972. Title IX, an amendment to the federal Education Act, states:

No person in the United States shall, on the basis of sex, be excluded from participation in, be denied the benefits of, or be subjected to discrimination under any educational program or activity receiving Federal financial assistance.

This law applies to elementary and secondary public schools; some twenty-seven thousand colleges and universities; and all other schools and training centers that receive federal money. Title IX covers a broad sweep. It says that schools and training programs cannot discriminate in terms of admissions, financial aid, student housing, counseling courses, health care, extracurricular activities, or in hiring and salary practices. Students, parents, school employees, and employee unions are all covered by the law.

An example of how Title IX works can be found in physical education requirements, which were spelled out in 1978. These rules say that female students are entitled to equal opportunity in sports. Schools are supposed to provide coeducational gym classes, except for contact sports such as football, hockey, and wrestling. In noncontact sports such as baseball, if there is only one team representing the school, both boys and girls must be allowed to try for the team.

The trouble with Title IX is that it was not necessarily understood by the people whose rights were supposed to be protected. The Women's Rights Committee of the American Federation of Teachers (AFL-CIO) found that even teachers were poorly schooled in Title IX. To help them analyze their own situations, the committee designed a questionnaire for teachers to apply to their school. Sample questions included, Are salaries for male and female teachers who hold the same position equal? Are after-school jobs available to both boys and girls on an equal basis? Are all courses open to all students (allowing for separate sex education classes)? Are males and females disciplined in the same way when they break rules? Do dress code requirements differ on the basis of sex? Answering no to any of these questions meant that Title IX was being violated.

Teachers were advised that the local school or school board was supposed to provide a grievance process for complaints. (This is usually a committee that listens to evidence and orders changes if the complaint is found to be true.) Teachers were also urged to see that antidiscrimination provisions were written into their union contracts with the local school board.

While Title IX seemed like a good enough plan for ending discrimination, it still depended on the intentions of individual school districts and watchdog activity by individual teachers and teacher unions. And when no local remedy was available, complaints had to go to the federal agency charged with enforcement of Title IX. In this case, the agency is the Department of Education. The agency has never used its most potent weapon to enforce a decision against an offending institution; it has never cut off federal funds to a school that fails to live up to Title IX.

The advantage of the ERA when facing problems such as Title IX enforcement is that the ERA does not depend on a single agency like the Department of Education to uphold the law. Under the ERA, state legislatures and courts could also make changes. The legislatures can write new laws in the states' educational codes. The courts can hear cases brought by individuals or groups against the schools. With more ways to air complaints, there would be new policies in areas where school administrators have either been ignorant of the law or have hoped to get by without being seriously challenged.

Family law, governing marriage, divorce, personal property, and child custody, often treats men and women differently, depending on the states in which they live. Some states still have laws based on ideas that date back to colonial times. In Georgia, the old idea that husband and wife are one unit—and that unit is the husband—persisted in state law until recently. Up to 1974, Georgia law declared, "The husband is the head of the family and the wife is subject to him; her legal existence is merged in the husband, except so far as the law recognizes her separately, either for her own protection, or for her benefit, or for the preservation of the public order."

Such laws put a woman at the mercy of her husband's or a judge's goodwill. With a woman's low income-earning capacity and a man's legal right to control family property and income, a woman can become poor at any time, no matter what she has contributed to family life. (Women have a fifty-fifty chance of being divorced, separated, or widowed by the time they reach middle age.) What happens to married women economically depends in great part on marriage and inheritance laws. State laws determine who owns personal property, the conditions of financial support, the terms of child custody, and financial arrangements in the case of divorce. Personal property includes everything from jewelry to houses, boats, bank accounts, land, clothing, and household furnishings.

In forty-two states and the District of Columbia there are Separate Property laws. Under these, the earnings of each spouse belong solely to that person, as does any property brought into the marriage or inherited during the marriage. Eight states have Community Property laws: Arizona, California, Idaho, Louisiana, Nevada, New Mexico, Texas, and Washington. Under these laws, each spouse has joint ownership in the earnings of the other, with each having the right to own and control separately any property brought to the marriage or inherited during it.

While the courts rarely have anything to do with a marriage that is together, property rights are frequently decided when a marriage falls apart.

In states with Separate Property laws, a woman has no right to any assets acquired through her husband's earnings, although half of these states do ask for a fair property settlement. In most cases of divorce, the husband—who is nearly always the main breadwinner—can give the wife as much or as little material security as he pleases. In a divorce where the woman has been a full-time homemaker, she will be especially vulnerable. Alimony, which is supposed to compensate a homemaker for the lack of income during marriage, is awarded in less than 15 percent of all divorce cases. In more than half of these cases it is never paid.

Family law also decides what happens to property after the death of a spouse. When a husband dies first, what the widow is entitled to varies widely depending upon the state. In Community Property states, a widow can inherit half of all property acquired during the marriage, regardless of what a written will says. But in Separate Property states, a widow's inheritance can range from nothing at all to a one-third or one-half interest in the estate, with no right to give it to whomever she chooses upon her own death. In Separate Property states women who die before their husbands are not entitled to leave any marital property whatsoever. All comes under the control of the surviving husband.

Such marriage laws may well be changed under the influence of the ERA. According to the League of Women Voters, "the experience in states with state ERAs (such as Pennsylvania, Montana and New Mexico) suggests that ratification of the ERA could lead to increased financial security for the divorced or widowed woman, by encouraging a trend toward reform of the state marital property laws."

In Ohio, an ERA Task Force recommended that divorce settlements should take into account the age and education of the partners, their different job skills, who will have child custody, any physical or mental disabilities in the family, and the financial resources of both husband and wife. If the homemaking spouse has not worked outside the home, the courts would have to honor the contribution she or he made, along with the fact that this partner may be unskilled and unable to compete in the labor market. It was recommended that dependent men be given as much consideration as dependent women.

A wide variety of practices would be affected by the ERA. Women and men could sue for divorce on the same grounds. For example, if leaving the home was considered "desertion" by a wife, the same charge could be raised if the husband left. Men would be entitled to alimony. And it could no longer be assumed that women should be favored over men in child custody cases. Both parents would have to be considered on individual merits. States could no longer insist that a woman take a man's name upon marriage—a custom related to the idea of a wife being a husband's property.

Finally, the ERA would challenge laws that control a married woman's legal residence. Such laws have led to illogical situations. For instance, some states have insisted that a woman is a resident of whatever state her husband claims. As an example, the wife of a sailor may live in California. But if her husband joined the Navy in Florida, she is not entitled to vote in California even if it is her home state. She is supposed to vote an absentee ballot in Florida even though she has never lived in Florida and knows nothing about the state. Under the ERA, a woman could claim her own state of residence, which would allow her to vote in that state and to receive benefits such as resident tuition at state schools.

Insurance of all kinds, including life, health, disability, and automobile insurance, is openly based on discriminatory practices. "All premiums are predicated on discrimination," said George K. Bernstein, speaking for the American Insurance Association, "and without it, policyholders would pay the same rate regardless of their risk characteristics."

The trouble lies in sex being used as a deciding factor in setting rates. In the case of life insurance, no unique physical characteristic has been found that is related to length of life in one sex but not in the other. But because women on the average tend to live longer than men they are required to pay more for life insurance. In respect to automobile insurance, companies in many states charge higher rates for young men than for young women regardless of how many safe miles the individual applicant has driven. In the case of health insurance, maternity benefits have been limited and often expensive, especially for single women. And disability insurance clearly favors male applicants. Women pay more than men, although health statistics show that women are absent from work because of illness or injury no more than men. For homemakers there is no easily available disability insurance. Running a home is not recognized as an occupation.

It seems likely that the ERA would be used to challenge insurance practices. While the federal government cannot regulate private insurance companies, the government's relationship to the states, and thereby state insurance commissions, may open the door to federal influence. Any attack against insurance practices on constitutional grounds would take place in the courts. Anticipating this, the AAUW study on the ERA states, "The principle underlying insurance is sharing—spreading among many the cost of coverage against a specific event to reduce that cost for all. ERA will require that a basis other than gender be found for sharing the cost of all types of insurance and pension protection."

Social Security benefits have been uneven for both women and men. While a married working woman pays Social Security taxes at the same rate as a working man, she gets less back from the program when she retires. If a wife dies or retires, her husband can draw on her Social Security only if he earned less than half the family's income. If a wife dies leaving dependent children, the children can draw on her Social Security, but not the husband. If the husband dies, both widow and children are entitled.

Under the ERA, married men and women would be entitled to the same benefits after age sixty-five. But the average benefit paid to a retired working woman would continue to be less than the average benefit paid to a working man because of the difference in male and female wages. The Social Security system reflects the earning status of women and cannot correct the results of discriminatory wage patterns. (The average monthly Social Security payment to women in 1979 was $230, compared to $339 for men.)

The ERA would also have no effect on some of the other problems in the Social Security system. There is no coverage for a homemaker in her or his own right. A woman who has taken care of a house and children will continue to receive benefits based on whatever her husband paid into the system. If she is widowed before age sixty, unless she is handicapped or has dependents there will be no benefits until she reaches sixty. If she is divorced before the twentieth year of marriage, she will get no benefits based on her former husband's contribution to the system.

THE POWER OF THE ERA

"Social security legislation is replete with sex discrimination," Congresswoman Margaret Heckler told the International Women's Year Conference in 1977. While married women contribute billions of dollars to the system, they realize few benefits. Heckler also pointed to other problems facing women—the enormous backlog of cases before the EEOC (130,000); and the way the Equal Credit Opportunity Act was not being enforced.

Such laws are incomplete solutions, anyway, she said. What is needed is a major remedy:

Comparing the ERA with these piecemeal solutions reminds me of the beginnings of the age of flight when individuals first attempted to fly, strapping wings to their backs, flapping their arms, inventing contraptions which they felt would enable them to soar, like the creatures of the air. But these devices barely got off the ground. It was only when the inventors added the engine—the power—to the emerging structure that the flying machine began to succeed. The surge of power propelling the wings lifted it up, above the forces that held it earthbound.

The Equal Rights Amendment is the power of constitutional protection that will allow women's equality to become airborne. Without the ERA women's equality will continue to flap its wings, making small leaps forward, struggling against the forces that hold us down. With the ERA, we will have the power, the constitutional foundation to soar above our current limitations, limitations which have bound us to limited choice of opportunity....

A country that can put men on the moon can put women in the Constitution. If we really believe in the inscription engraved on the Supreme Court building, equal justice under the law, the ERA is the only way to achieve it.

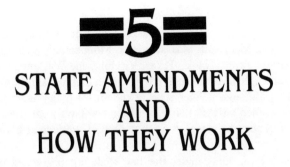

STATE AMENDMENTS
AND
HOW THEY WORK

Ti-Grace Atkinson, a leader of NOW when it was formed, broke from the group in 1968 because it was too tame for her. Atkinson wanted to see more radical action within the women's movement, with women refusing to compromise in cases of social injustice. For instance, Atkinson wanted women to stop getting married. She called marriage slavery. "If you look at the laws," she said, "it is legalized rape, causes unpaid labor, curtails a woman's freedom of movement and requires no assurances of love from a man." Atkinson may have been correct in how marital laws can oppress women, but very few people wanted to get rid of marriage to correct the problem. That would be like throwing out the baby with the bath water; the water may be dirty, but the baby has its good points.

Most equal rights supporters were more moderate and used to dealing with problems in traditional ways. They expected to use the law to change the law. While the federal ERA gathered support, state equal rights amendments affecting such subjects as marriage, divorce, education, and employment were being adopted in many parts of the country. State ERAs provide the foundation for overhauling state and local laws that discriminate on the basis of sex. They also serve as a model for what could happen under a federal ERA.

Fourteen states added equal rights provisions to their constitutions between 1971 and 1976: Alaska, Colorado, Connecticut, Hawaii, Illinois, Maryland, Massachusetts, Montana, New Hampshire, New Mexico, Pennsylvania, Texas, Virginia, and Washington. (Wyoming and Utah have had such provisions in their constitutions since the 1890s, although neither state is known for being aggressive in securing women's rights.) Nine of the states' laws were worded the same, or almost the same, as Section One of the federal ERA:

> Equality of rights under the law shall not be denied or abridged by the United States or by any State on account of sex.

Under a state ERA, any state laws or regulations that discriminate on the basis of sex can be changed or thrown out by the legislature and courts. The Women's Law Project and the NOW Legal Defense and Education Fund—research organizations devoted to studying legal issues affecting women and lobbying for specific causes—surveyed the results of state equal rights provisions and published their findings in 1982. The ERA Impact Project, as the report was called, reached four main conclusions about the results of state ERAs.

First, it was found that ERAs are effective. "State ERAs have produced an expansion of rights that has greatly benefited women, who traditionally have been the victims of laws and governmental practices that made them second-class citizens with second-class rights."

For the first time in Pennsylvania, for example, a state supreme court decision based on the ERA gave wives some ownership of household items, even if they were paid for by the husband's wages. Under the old Pennsylvania law, the wage earner was the sole owner of household property, including everything from the doormat to the covers on the bed. State ERAs also extended rights that were formerly limited to one sex to both men and women, thus improving the legal status of all. In New Mexico and Texas child custody laws were amended to give custody to whichever parent could serve the child's best interests.

Second, state ERAs created momentum to reform the whole list of sex-biased state laws—not just those that are challenged. This reform takes place in the regular business of a state legislature; the need to use the courts to file complaints about discrimination has therefore been lessened or eliminated. Court cases are costly for both the government and the complainant, involving extensive legal and clerical work with high fees for most professionals, such as lawyers, involved. An overloaded court calender can also lead to long waiting periods for the parties in a grievance, keeping a case on hold for months or even for years.

Third, it was found that six states have made the greatest progress under state equal rights legislation: Colorado, Maryland, Massachusetts, New Mexico, Pennsylvania, and Washington. All have equal rights laws that closely parallel the proposed federal ERA.

Fourth, the most significant gains in legal rights under state ERAs are in the areas of *employment, education,* and *family law.*

In *employment,* restrictions on overtime hours for women, restrictions on the kinds of jobs they can perform, unequal pay practices, and unequal employment benefits have all been challenged under state ERAs. For example, in Connecticut and Illinois, limits on the numbers of hours women can work have been repealed, which opens up wider job opportunities. In Hawaii, a pregnant woman can no longer be disqualified for unemployment benefits. In Maryland, women can now work as state police and fire fighters, drawing equal salaries and benefits. In Washington, the state ERA is being used to challenge unequal college athletics programs. Women's coaches have filed suit because of unequal pay and other terms of employment. Pennsylvania has altered a variety of laws. It has dropped a minimum height requirement for state police officers. Girls can now be newspaper carriers and women can be barbers. There are no more discriminatory "Help Wanted" ads. Parole officers are now assigned according to their ability to function well in a particular environment, rather than on the basis of sex alone.

In the area of *education* the ERA Impact Project found that state ERAs are doing a better job challenging discrimination in the schools than either Title IX of the federal Education Act or the equal protection clause of the Fourteenth Amendment, because education falls mostly under state, not federal, control. For example, under the New Mexico ERA, it was ruled that girls could not be excluded from a special high school vocational program. In Texas, a university was required to provide men and women with equal housing on campus. It was also found that a rule allowing men to live off campus while denying women the same right violated the Texas ERA. In Massachusetts, female law students won the right to apply for scholarship aid previously available only to males. In Pennsylvania, the ERA helped girls win the right to compete in interscholastic sports.

New principles of fairness are also being established under state ERAs in the area of *family law*. Support payments, alimony, and child custody are being treated differently than in the past. According to the ERA Impact Project, "State ERAs are being interpreted to support the view that marriage is an economic, as well as a social and emotional partnership. As a result, married women, especially homemakers, have acquired new rights." Legal responsibility for meeting the needs of the whole family is to be shared by both husband and wife, according to their ability to meet those needs. If a man has good wage-earning ability and a woman is a homemaker with no other job experience, this must be considered if they separate or divorce. If a woman is the chief breadwinner, the man is entitled to alimony.

In Pennsylvania, before the state ERA was in effect, a woman who was legally separated from her husband could not get support payments any larger than one-third of her husband's net income. After ERA, such laws were overturned. One judge said the old law showed "an ingrained sexist philosophy whereby a man's labor for money was somehow thought to be more valuable than a woman's work as a homemaker."

The courts also used state ERAs to establish the principle of shared responsibility for children. This furthered the idea that marriage is a partnership and that domestic responsibility is more than bringing home a paycheck.

The parent who has child custody and who devotes full time to child rearing is not forced by equal rights legislation to work outside the home. In Pennsylvania, a father claimed the ERA required his former wife to get a job to help pay the bills for the three young children in her custody. The court decided that the parent who is rearing the children must decide if they're going to be better off with a working parent or with a parent who is at home full time. Courts in other states reached similar conclusions.

Inheritance laws have also changed under state ERAs. In New Mexico, a woman can now will half of all jointly owned personal property to whomever she wishes. Before the new law, her half went automatically to her husband. In Montana, a husband's consent is no longer required to let a wife will her personal property as she chooses. In Pennsylvania, inheritance tax deductions for widows now apply to widowers, too.

All of the new laws described above have come about through changes in old laws, or by throwing out such laws altogether. But what criteria do courts and legislatures use to decide that a law is out of line with the state ERA and must be changed? According to the ERA Impact Project, there should be a "Yes" answer to two specific questions:

(1) Does the challenged law or practice involve governmental action?

(2) Does the challenged law or practice treat men and women unequally?

In respect to the first question, every court that has been asked to define the influence of a state ERA has said it applies only to government action. The actions of private individuals, businesses, or institutions are not in the province of state ERAs. The "state action requirement," however, can be more broad than is supposed. In Washington, for example, interscholastic athletic association rules have to provide equal opportunity for both boys and girls because the association is supported by schools, which in turn receive state funds.

In respect to the second question, the ERA Impact Project says there are two ways to decide whether a law or practice treats men and women unequally. First, is the law or regulation written in sex-based language? Does it say, for example, "No woman may work after 10:00 p.m. in an establishment selling food or liquor." Or, "Dormitories at the state university shall be available to first-year male students and first- through fourth-year female students." Such language clearly shows discrimination. But, secondly, even without sex-based language the law can still have the *effect* of classifying people and thereby discriminate on the basis of sex. For example, a law may forbid unemployment compensation payments to a worker who quits a job in order to follow their spouse to a new residence. The sex of the worker is never mentioned in the unemployment compensation law. But when the law is applied, it is found that women are overwhelmingly those who are hurt by the law. As a class of people they are being prevented from receiving such benefits, even though they paid part of their wages into the unemployment compensation system. (In California, it was found that 99 percent of such applicants who were denied unemployment benefits were women.)

When a court finds that the state ERA is being violated, there are two possible remedies. It can throw out the law or it can extend the law to cover both men and women. If the law is considered beneficial to those covered, the court will usually extend it to cover both sexes. For example, in Washington, only husbands could sue for loss of their spouse's affection and support (consortium). The Washington State Supreme Court ruled that women now also have the right to sue on these grounds.

In the case of laws that prohibit some type of action, the courts have generally invalidated them. For example, in Pennsylvania it was decided that a law against hiring girls as newspaper carriers was illegal, and the law was struck down.

While lawsuits are one way to identify and correct unfair government practices, there is a more efficient method. The legislature can reform laws as part of its regular business. Creating a state commission to review the legal status of women can aid in the task. In many states, such commissions already exist. In Pennsylvania, the Commission for Women drafted twenty-six bills for legislative approval which would bring state laws into line with the state ERA. Nineteen of these bills passed quickly and the legislature is reviewing the rest. This kind of coordinated, comprehensive reform has made many separate court challenges unnecessary.

But the League of Women Voters warns against the idea that state ERAs can settle problems of inequality for women nationwide. Only about one-third of the states have so far included equal rights for women in their constitutions. Beyond that, unless the legislatures choose to rewrite discriminatory laws, it is up to state courts to interpret equal rights. And judges vary widely in their interpretations of equality. LWV wants to see "a single, uniform federal standard for judging sex discrimination cases" rather than the different standards that exist state to state.

Women who feel confident of equal treatment under the law in their home states may have only to cross a state border to lose valuable rights.

OPPOSITION TO
THE ERA

When the final deadline for ratification of the Equal Rights Amendment was reached in June 1982, without its being approved by thirty-eight state legislatures as required, opponents of the measure were elated. A big party was held in Washington, D.C., to honor forty-five men and nine women who helped defeat the ERA. One speaker compared the victory to the way Israel's prime minister was thrashing the Palestine Liberation Organization. *Conservative Digest* Editor John Lofton said, "I salute you fellows for doing to the ERA what Menachem Begin is doing to the P.L.O." "Special service" awards for trouncing the ERA were given to the leader of the Moral Majority, the Reverend Jerry Falwell, and to conservative politicians Undersecretary of State James Buckley and Senator Jesse Helms.

The opposition had blocked ratification in fifteen state legislatures. They had organized efforts to rescind approval in five other states. All of this in spite of a 1980 poll which showed 58 percent of Americans favored the ERA and only 31 percent were against it.

Who were the anti-ERA forces who convinced state legislators to block passage of the Twenty-seventh Amendment to the Constitution? Did they really believe the ERA was not in the best interests of the women of America?

Overall, the move to defeat the ERA was the work of a coalition of conservative citizens. There were homemakers from the suburbs; working women from offices and factories; politicians, such as Jesse Helms, from the South; members of religious groups who strictly interpret scripture and church rules—fundamentalist Christians, Mormons, Orthodox Jews, and conservative Roman Catholics; some lawyers; and members of special groups opposed to progressive ideas and legislation. The best known of these groups was the Moral Majority, a patriotic organization whose ideals depend on a traditional family system with "father" in the world and "mother" in the home; the John Birch Society, a "watchdog" group that speaks out against liberal legislation and trends; and the Eagle Forum and Stop-ERA groups formed especially to fight the Amendment.

Opposition to the ERA was explained in both logical and emotional terms. The first kind of argument centered on how the Amendment would be interpreted. For instance, it was felt that giving the Supreme Court and federal agencies authority to spell out the meaning of equal rights would be risky. Decisions made on such a level would be too far removed from the ideas and desires of the people. These critics of the ERA said equal rights should be secured on local and state levels, where unpopular decisions could be overturned by the people through referendums and by voting legislators out of office.

The second kind of argument was based on a desire to prevent changes in existing social customs, especially in "masculine" and "feminine" roles. These critics of the ERA worried about the loss of privacy and unisex bathrooms. They said the Amendment would reinforce constitutionalized abortion; it would destroy protective labor legislation; it would legalize homosexual marriage; it would take away a man's responsibility to support his wife and children. Conservative churches feared the ERA would require them to accept women into the ministry on the same basis as men. The possibility of women being drafted was a heated issue. What if women became prisoners of war? What if mothers had to pick up rifles and leave their babies at home?

Many women who worked in factories and at other blue-collar jobs thought the ERA was of no use to them. The idea of equal rights was viewed as a kind of fringe benefit for middle-class women who already had a lot of privileges by comparison to those in a lower economic class. Women living on meager incomes were not impressed by arguments about other women having the right to win law school scholarships or to compete for management jobs. Many feared the ERA would hurt them. They believed it would mean the loss of the little bit of child support or welfare payments they counted on to make the difference between getting by or living in poverty. They had too little experience with good fortune to question the narrow conditions of their lives. Asked why she opposed the ERA, a factory worker pointed out that at the supermarket all the checkers were women and the managers men. "That's how it is and how it will always be," she said.

Not all of the so-called privileged class of women believed the ERA was for them, either. College women who planned on "landing a good catch" and being full-time wives and mothers feared a federal equal rights mandate. They understood the ERA to mean that they would *have* to work and give up their children to federally managed day-care centers. Some imagined they would have to keep working even if they were pregnant and sick. They also saw a danger to male/ female relationships in building an outside career. It was assumed that any husband would resent a successful working wife, so it was folly to plan for a serious career or to insist on equal rights. "We will never be equal. We might as well be safe," a twenty-year-old ERA opponent said.

Such feelings of vulnerability and dependency were being exploited by the real powers behind the anti-ERA campaign, ERA supporters said. Financial and moral support to stop the ERA were believed to come primarily from business and political factions with a stake in social conditions remaining as they are—with low wages for women and with men setting the rules and running the country. According to Betty Friedan, "It is a conspiracy of those whose power, or profit, rests on the manipulation of the fears...of passive women."

The insurance and textile industries had strong financial reasons for defeating the Amendment. A change in existing practices could cut deeply into their profits. Some feminists believed the insurance industry, in particular, was playing the same role in this fight that the liquor lobby had played in blocking the drive for women's suffrage. The president of NOW, Eleanor Smeal, told *Social Education* magazine:

The insurance industry has one of the largest lobbies in the state legislatures. It is an industry whose commodity discriminates on the basis of sex and profits by doing so. Rates, benefits, premiums, and annuities all have sex-based rating systems. Believe me, on that basis, the house always wins. The insurance lobbyists have been vigorously fighting the elimination of sex discrimination in their policies.

The textile industry hires many more women than men and routinely underpays them, according to Smeal. It is no coincidence that the South—the heart of the textile industry—stood squarely against ratification. Smeal said that women working to defeat ERA were being used as pawns by such business interests:

> People who profit from sex discrimination would like to keep the laws as weak as they can; they use their lobbying power and influence to maintain the *status quo* at the expense of American women.

A desire to keep the status quo—the existing state of affairs— motivated much of the opposition to the ERA, including the opinions of anti-ERA lawyers. Legal opposition to the Amendment came from old, conservative roots in the legal profession, and mostly from male lawyers. (In California, 48 percent of male lawyers opposed ratification, while only 13 percent of female lawyers opposed it.)

Rex Lee, dean of the law school of Brigham Young University, which is affiliated with the Mormon Church, warned that the ERA could overturn laws that allow distinctions between men and women. He said the ERA would bring in "a parade of horribles," such as unisex toilets, women in combat service, the destruction of laws protecting homemakers, and the loss of preferred treatment for mothers in child custody cases. While other lawyers said the Amendment would not mean loss of privacy or homosexual marriages, Lee said they are missing the point. "No one can say how the ERA will be interpreted. . . . The real question is, since there is a risk of these things happening, is there enough of a need for a new light to search out discriminatory practices? My answer is a resounding 'No.'" Professor Lee said the due process clause of the Fourteenth Amendment is sufficient to correct any wrongs.

Another legal expert, Professor Paul Freund of Harvard University, also called for increased use of the Fourteenth Amendment, which was ratified in 1868, rather than adoption of another amendment which outlaws discrimination specifically on the basis of sex.

The equal protection clause of the Fourteenth Amendment, which was meant by Congress to deal with discrimination on account of race or former condition of servitude, states:

No state shall make or enforce any law which shall abridge the privileges or immunities of citizens of the United States, nor shall any State deprive any person of life, liberty, or property, without due process of law; nor deny to any person within its jurisdiction the equal protection of the laws.

Freund said the number of sex discrimination cases which have been tried under the Fourteenth Amendment is small because the amendment simply hasn't been used. Women are to blame for part of this, he said. The lack of use of the Fourteenth "can be ascribed partly to the failure of women's groups to mount a series of selected test cases challenging forms of discrimination and in part to the fact that some discriminatory laws have been invalidated by lower courts without further appeal."

Some legal experts called the ERA a "blank check"—too open and too loose. They worried that the lack of specific guidelines to define discrimination would create confusion in the courts. Such questions as when a protective law is a benefit and when it is a liability would not be clear. Professor Philip Kurland of the University of Chicago said that such questions should be settled through specific legislation. He said that "equality of the sexes" is a magical phrase with only symbolic value. The professor pointed out that all women do not want to compete on an equal basis with men or to lose any special legal rights they may now have.

Not only women stand to lose prerogatives under the ERA, according to its foes. Supporters of states' rights feared expansion of federal powers under the Amendment. Senator Sam Ervin told Congress the ERA "would virtually reduce the states of this union to meaningless zeros on the nation's map." Beverly Campbell, an anti-ERA activist in Virginia, also objected to the second section of the Amendment, which gives Congress the authority to pass laws enforcing it. "At the state level, people can vote for a change of lawmakers, or have a referendum election. But you can't change anything at the federal level." Rosemary Thompson, Illinois director of the Eagle Forum, said, "The real concern is that the federal government would come and tell states that all of the laws must comply with what they think. Illinois has a fine equal protection law that allows equal opportunity, but also a reasonable distinction between men and women." State legislators opposing the ERA said that each legislature must decide individually whether the concepts found in such a law are necessary for the citizens of its state.

While legislators, lawyers, professors, and public figures argued the wisdom of the ERA, the women who expected to be affected by it responded more directly. Feeling threatened by a law they were told would force them to get jobs and take away their husbands' responsibility to provide support, homemakers who opposed the ERA took their case to the state capitols. In Tallahassee, Florida, women lobbying to defeat ratification gave their representatives jars of homemade jelly. The gift tags read: *Preserve the family unit.* In Illinois, women went to Springfield carrying loaves of freshly baked bread for the male lawmakers. Their slogan: *From the bread-maker to the bread-winner.* The message the women carried was always the same, "Don't make us change our lives."

Critics of this conservative point of view theorized that it represents fear; fear rising from the very real dependence of women in a male-dominated society, where women have been raised to "be pretty, be good, and don't make trouble." Andrea Dworkin, a feminist writer, said that "Subservience to male wishes becomes the meaning of a woman's life." In her book *Right-Wing Women*, she said women hang on to traditional female roles because of fear. What will happen if a woman rebels and refuses to be a servantlike wife and mother? Dworkin said women may not know it with their conscious minds, but they fear that if they refuse to play the expected roles they risk being battered physically or emotionally, going mad, or even dying from the insecurity of having to create a new identity. Survival for such women depends on conforming. To be safe in a man's world, a woman must even ignore what happens to other women, she said.

In the ERA controversy, the idea that women were already protected by the law and that they stood to lose under the Amendment was particularly strong in the *Old South* (former slave-owning states with a tradition of "taking care of" subservient members of society). North Carolina Senator Sam Ervin forecast nothing less than disaster when the ERA was introduced into Congress. He said it would mean the end of femininity and the American family. In 1973, *The New York Times Magazine* reviewed Ervin's fight against ERA:

... fired by his quarrel with ERA's vagueness and also by a stirring expression of reverence for his own beloved mother and his wife, [he] tried valiantly, and unsuccessfully, to tack amendments onto ERA that would have retained protections and exemptions in the law for women, reaffirmed fathers' responsibility for support of their children, upheld laws securing privacy to men and women or boys and girls, retained laws punishing sex crimes and protected Federal and State laws making distinctions between legal rights of men and women when the distinction is based on physiological or functional differences.

Ervin's amendments were defeated, but what he said was echoed by legislators in state capitols. In a debate in Tallahassee, Florida, in 1977, State Senator Dave McClain said that differences between men and women make some equal options, such as shared military service, out of the question. "Man has the physical strength. Man has got it. *God* decreed that. I didn't, you didn't. And God decreed that women would have the children."

The idea that God's plan for human nature was being violated by the ERA was also expressed by fundamentalist preachers, who worried that the Amendment would legalize homosexuality. The *Yale Law Review* report on the ERA had said the Amendment would have nothing to do with laws regarding homosexuals. The only connection would be that if a state legalized marriage between members of one sex, then it would have to allow marriage between members of the other sex, too. Nevertheless, the ERA and homosexuality were seen as parts of the same problem of growing immorality. A fundamentalist preacher and conservative leader, the Reverend Jerry Falwell, wrote in his book *Listen America!*, "Feminists desire to eliminate God-given differences that exist between the sexes; that is why they are pro-homosexual and lesbian."

This attitude was widespread among religious conservatives. In Miami, a city ordinance describing homosexual rights was seen as proof that ERA supporters were taking over the political system. "Families" made up of all-male or all-female couples were considered a crime against nature and a deep insult to the traditional American way of life. Church magazines and newsletters were centered on these emotional issues; congregations met to plan ways to stop liberal trends, like the ERA, that were supposed to be ruining America.

Not only Southern fundamentalists opposed the Amendment. Another religious group with money and human resources to put into the fight was the Church of Jesus Christ of Latter Day Saints—the Mormon Church. Mormons are headquartered in the state of Utah, but dispersed throughout the Northwest and other parts of the country. They operate on a strict patriarchal system, with a line of male leaders who regulate all aspects of members' lives including the activities of women. Mormon opposition to the ERA was based on God's plan as interpreted by male clergy. God meant male and female differences to last to eternity, they said. ERA would challenge male authority and upset the father's position in the family. "We recognize men and women as equally important before the Lord, but with differences biologically, emotionally, and in other ways," the church president said. Mormon women opposed ERA because it would destroy legal safeguards protecting women, children, and the home. They were told how to work against the Amendment, and their testimony against it in state legislatures was especially well organized and extensive.

Along with Mormons and other fundamentalist Protestants, opponents of the ERA were found in the Roman Catholic Church. While there were Catholics who lobbied for the Amendment, some volunteer service organizations within the Church, like the Knights of Columbus, vehemently opposed it. Catholic conservatives feared the Amendment would aid abortion, even though legal experts said abortion was a totally separate issue from ERA since it applies only to women and has nothing to do with equality of the sexes. Those conservatives, nevertheless, believed it would provide a constitutional basis for legalizing abortion.

Other groups fighting the ERA were the John Birch Society, a political faction deeply disturbed by liberal economic and social changes; the State Federation of Farm Bureaus, a conservative rural organization; the Daughters of the American Revolution, women who take pride in tracing their families to the Founding Fathers; the Christian Anticommunism Crusade, a group dedicated to exposing trends that threaten democracy as they define it; the Ku Klux Klan, a secret society devoted to white male rule; the Veterans of Foreign Wars, a fraternity of ex-servicemen; the Moral Majority, an organization claiming to speak for all right-thinking citizens; and conservative wings of national organizations such as the American Legion and the Lutheran Church (which, like other large denominations, has differing branches). What these groups have in common is an ideology that is often called right-wing.

The "right" is a label that is applied to a range of conservative political views. Right-wing thinkers defend capitalism and reject any aspects of socialism, accepting the fact that some people are born with, or are given, extra advantages that lead them to success. Right-wing philosophy rejects government interference in various aspects of life such as business or education. Busing children to schools to achieve integration was violently opposed by right-wing groups.

The Moral Majority is an extreme right-wing organization that spells out its goals for the public. For instance, in a series of full-page advertisements in the *Anchorage Times* in 1981, Moral Majority of Alaska, Inc., described its reasons for existence. The organization favored a whole list of essentially conservative values: "pro-life" (against abortion), "pro-morality" (against nontraditional life-styles and for the Ten Commandments), "pro-America" (for the ideals expressed in 1776), and "pro-Alaska" (for getting the federal government out of the state as much as possible). The ads explained why members of the Moral Majority were "pro-family"—a concept that was used by many right-wing groups to attack the ERA. The reasoning was that women were being forced to work because of government interference in daily life.

> We have seen the government do its very best to undermine the family and its authority. This is evident in everything from education to attempted elimination of sex roles, allowing an economy to come into existence which forces both partners in a marriage to enter the work force in order to earn enough money just to survive. That greatly reduces the precious time available for parents to spend with their children.

While the leaders of various organizations like the Moral Majority were busy at a grass-roots level rousing public opinion against legislation like the ERA, one individual stood out above the rest. Phyllis Schlafly was honored by all as the founder, inspiration, and guiding light of the "Stop-ERA" movement. Everyone who worked *for* the ERA said that if Schlafly had been on their side, the ERA would never have been defeated; it was she who turned the tide and sank the Amendment when victory seemed assured.

Schlafly headed a "pro-family" conference in Houston that opposed the International Women's Year Conference; she published the *Phyllis Schlafly Report*, a scholarly monthly newsletter full of opinions and information on topics such as "What's Wrong with Equal Rights for Women"; she founded a conservative women's organization, the Eagle Forum, which she called "the alternative to Women's Lib." She was a network radio commentator, a newspaper columnist, a wife, the mother of six children, and a lawyer, a degree she earned during the campaign to defeat the Amendment.

Schlafly liked to say that being a mother was her primary career, but from the time her first child was still in diapers, she traveled frequently, organizing, lobbying, and campaigning for causes she believed in. She ran for Congress twice from her home district in Illinois, and once for the office of president of the National Federation of Republican Women, an arm of the Republican Party. (Some believed that losing these elections motivated her to seek political power as head of the anti-ERA campaign.) As an author, she wrote about foreign policy and national defense; a book promoting the presidential candidacy of Senator Barry Goldwater in 1964; the story of a Roman Catholic cardinal who exemplified her own Catholic religious principles; and an anti-feminist book, *The Power of the Positive Woman*. All her talents were finally centered in Stop-ERA, the name for both the campaign and a network of nationwide committees that she controlled from her home in Alton, Illinois.

If Senator Sam Ervin's amendments had passed the Senate, Schlafly said she could have accepted the ERA. But she hated the power the Amendment gave federal authorities to rewrite state laws if they didn't conform to ERA standards. She opposed women being drafted, and as a critic of national defense policies she pointed out that the United States would be weakened by females in the armed services while the Soviets stayed strong with less than one percent female soldiers. And like Ervin, she ignored the Senate testimony which ruled out a mandate for homosexual marriages and showed how abortion would not be affected by the Amendment. She insisted the ERA would pave the way for homosexuals to marry and adopt children. She also said the ERA would give women a constitutional right to abortion—because they would demand an equal right with men not to be pregnant. But all in all, the Amendment would take away rights, not confer them, she said. Financial support for wives and minor children and the assurance of a home would be lost.

Schlafly liked to characterize pro-ERA activists as discontented women, spoiled by all the benefits they already possessed and obsessed with the idea of personal power. She said that the oppression of women exists "only in their distorted minds." She said, "The U.S. Constitution is not the place for symbols or slogans, it is not the proper device to alleviate psychological problems of personal inferiority. Symbols and slogans belong on bumper strips—not in the Constitution. It would be a tragic mistake for our nation to succumb to the tirades and demands of a few women who are seeking a constitutional cure for their personal problems."

Schlafly's work as the chief opponent of the ERA brought her recognition at a time when the most rigid social and political conservatives claimed they were being ignored. The "silent majority" said that the liberal press paid attention only to other liberals, that they ignored the true majority of Americans who they claimed were conservative in the same sense that they were. Phyllis Schlafly was seen as a valuable exception to the rule; she knew how to get media attention and how to express ultra-conservative opinions in a way that captured headlines.

Journalist Carol Felsenthal described Schlafly's leadership qualities in a 1981 biography, *The Sweetheart of the Silent Majority*. Felsenthal was impressed by Schlafly's confidence, energy, sense of humor, and lack of vanity. She admired how cool Schlafly was in hot situations. She saw her spat upon at the IWY conference in Houston, and not flinching. Felsenthal said people either idolized or despised Schlafly; she created strong emotions. In turn, Schlafly saw the world in plain terms: moral and immoral, with good guys and bad guys and nobody in between.

Schlafly told the good guys in her world to be proud of playing supportive roles in their families and of being dedicated homemakers. Schlafly praised traditional feminine virtues in her book *The Power of the Positive Woman*, and attacked equal rights legislation and feminism.

Ignoring the fact that many feminists supported homemaking as an honorable vocation and were working to get homemakers more financial security, Schlafly insisted that the women's movement "deliberately degrades the homemaker and hacks away at her sense of self-worth and pleasure in being female."

Schlafly also talked about "husband's rights." She said that a National Organization for Women's resolution on fair employment practice showed "hatred for husbands as family providers." The resolution read:

(Resolved) that NOW call on the EEOC (Equal Employment Opportunity Commission) to issue an immediate ruling prohibiting applications that require information on sex, including given name of applicant, and that NOW demand that the EEOC prohibit questions concerning marital or parental plans or status . . . from pre-employment inquiries of any sort.

Schlafly said if employers follow such guidelines, eliminating job preference for married men with dependents, "This is clear and cruel discrimination against a husband and father trying to support his family." The only men who could benefit from equal rights laws, especially the ERA, were offbeats and deadbeats, Schlafly told her readers. Equal rights legislation, especially the ERA, "will provide liberation for . . . the homosexual who wants the same rights as husbands . . . the husband who wants to escape supporting his wife and children . . . the coward who wants to get out of military service by giving his place to a woman."

Schlafly's knack for turning complex issues into simple black and white served her well. She would use whatever worked to catch the public eye—sentimental slogans or zany humor. At a rally in Springfield, Illinois, she shared the camera with a preacher in a gorilla suit wearing a sign that read, *Don't Monkey with the Constitution.* She was good at communication, and this made her effective in both press relations and within her Stop-ERA organization. She had a remarkable memory for names and details and made each local committee feel that their efforts were foremost in her mind. She was always available to her workers; they could call her for advice day or night.

It could be argued that Schlafly achieved a large, devoted following because of her excellent leadership skills. But just as important, she represented fixed values in the midst of a changing world. Schlafly said that most women were just fine as they were; they did not need to join the career race, or try to understand new technology, or struggle to create an identity independent of home and family. Schlafly calmed women's fears. She helped them believe if they did their best as wives and mothers, men would be loyal and grateful.

Across the country, anti-ERA workers told legislators to leave things as they were. Many workers wore red, meaning *Stop* ERA.

In the state capitols where the final contest over ratification took place, the women in red faced women in green from NOW and other feminist organizations. Green was to remind voters of economic discrimination and to signal *Go* on ERA. The women were dressed like cheerleaders in a contest over values.

On both sides the ERA had mobilized women in a manner and in numbers never before experienced in the politics of the United States. The far-reaching effects of the Constitution on individual lives was being seen.

SUPPORT
FOR
RATIFICATION

Women against women: that's how the ERA battle appeared when groups of volunteer lobbyists competed to get state legislators to vote their way on ratification. One group of women claimed the Amendment would destroy their lives, tearing apart home and family. The other group said the effects of the ERA were being misunderstood— it would mean *more* security for homemakers, not less, and women would be first-class citizens for the first time. Looking at each other in the halls of state capitols where they went to lobby the legislators, "red" anti-ERA and "green" pro-ERA workers realized they were not sisters cut of the same cloth. As women they were deeply divided in their ideas of how to deal with life.

To ERA opponents, ERA supporters looked suspiciously un-ladylike. "Some of these women look like truck drivers. They're not like most women, gentle and sweet and feminine," a Stop-ERA volunteer in the Florida capitol said of the pro-ERA delegation. Many of the pro-ERA volunteers wore plain hairdos, little makeup, green-and-white T-shirts, and jeans. (Most of the anti-ERA group wore red dresses and red hats, and carried red roses.) But the women in green could not be easily characterized. Some were housewives, just like many of the opposition; others were blue-collar and white-collar workers. They ranged in age from students to seniors; and behind the visible ranks of ERA activists, there was a broad field of support across the country.

In the early 1970s, shortly after passage of the Amendment by Congress, many different kinds of civic and political organizations raised their hands to endorse the ERA. The list of supporters included more than two hundred organizations, with interests as diverse as the American Bar Association, representing lawyers, and the American Home Economics Association, representing teachers and other experts in nutrition, consumer science, and domestic skills. Support for the ERA came from the Democratic National Party, the Republican National Party, the Girl Scouts of the U.S.A., the Ladies Auxiliary of Veterans of Foreign Wars, the National School Boards Association, and the United States Conference of Mayors, among others.

Union support for the ERA was also widespread. There were textile workers; government employees; educators; radio, television, and film artists; newspaper reporters; communications workers; bakers; insurance workers; painters; teamsters; engineers; retail clerks; transportation workers; rubber and plastic craft workers; and representatives from other branches of commerce and industry.

The ERA was endorsed by conservatives such as Senator Strom Thurmond, President Richard Nixon, and Governor George Wallace of Alabama. Three widely admired First Ladies stood up for the ERA: Rosalyn Carter, Betty Ford, and Lady Bird Johnson. Johnson said, "I once thought the women's movement belonged more to my daughters than to me. But I've come to know it belongs to women of all ages."

Phyllis Schlafly liked to say that ERA supporters were "feminist fanatics" and "radicals." While some advocates fit her description, most did not. Radicals are those who challenge established views in any field of human endeavor—whether art, religion, government, or science. Most radicals *do* want to throw out the baby with the bath water. They tend to press their ideas to the extreme. This was not true of the membership of the many service organizations that endorsed the ERA. These organizations were known for their stability and devotion to strengthening community life. Radical traits could not be assigned to members of the Association of Junior Leagues, a social organization with many charities, who worked hard to ratify the ERA. Nor to women in other community service organizations who pledged their support for ratification of the ERA, such as the

American Federation of Soroptimist Clubs, Saint Joan's International Alliance of the Catholic Church of America, B'nai B'rith Women, Delta Sigma Theta, or the National Council of Church Women.

Similarly, supporters of the ERA no more looked alike than did the "rainbow of women" who were in Houston in 1977. T-shirts and jeans were seen at rallies, but ERA supporters could not be identified by what they wore. Florynce Kennedy, a lawyer and black activist, was known for her flair in clothes. She couldn't see why a feminist was supposed to be dowdy. "Nail polish or false eyelashes isn't politics. If you have good politics, what you wear is irrelevant," Kennedy said.

Support for ratifying the Amendment came from representatives of different political ideologies. For instance, Libertarians believe that the less government the better. They do not trust its good intentions and are concerned about misuse of even the clearest of constitutional guarantees. Yet the Association of Libertarian Feminists urged passage of the ERA. Libertarian Joan Taylor Kennedy reasoned that the government was already regulating citizens' lives; the ERA would see to it that government did its job more fairly. "It is already interfering with *private* discrimination in every area of employment, pay, credit, and education; it sets the terms on which it will permit people to marry, divorce, and bring up children," she said. "These powers will not be added to or subtracted from by the ERA. It is only *governmental* discrimination that is still legal."

At some distance on the political spectrum from Libertarians are liberals—citizens who strongly believe that government should assume responsibility for society's problems such as poverty and discrimination. Liberals care about the underdog. They advocate the rights of racial and religious minorities, support civil liberties, and say the government must help people who lack political and economic power. Most liberals belong to the Democratic Party, but there are also liberal Republican Party members and a number of liberal independents who belong to neither major party. But whatever their affiliation, it is safe to say that most liberals supported the ERA.

From the liberal point of view, the fight for the ERA was unfinished business in the civil rights struggle. Transportation, housing, education, and employment had been opened up to racial minorities under civil rights legislation and court decisions in the 1960s. Now a further step was needed to secure rights for women. "People said you can't legislate equality, but you can. We know from experience that the law can be a guide. It can become the conscience of the people," said Carolyn Reed, executive dierctor of the National Committee on Household Employment. Minority women—such as the maids and household workers that Reed represented—were still vulnerable to discrimination without the full force of the Constitution behind civil rights legislation. An ERA victory seemed crucial to some minority leaders.

Aileen Hernandez, an Hispanic business leader, warned, "A defeat of the ERA would be double or triple for minority women because we are in double and triple jeopardy, being women, minority, and, in most cases, poor."

Nationwide, minority women compose the largest pool of cheap labor. It is they who take whatever work they can get: picking crops, plucking poultry, cleaning fish, and doing dozens of unskilled assembly line jobs. With dependent children to care for, limited education, and no knowledge of skilled trades, most minority women are compelled to take poorly paid jobs without benefits. They need the protection of the law to compete for better jobs, obtain credit, and to pursue job training and education. The ERA promised to reinforce existing civil rights laws that would help women get education and employment opportunities. It also offered a fixed constitutional guarantee in case a particular Congress or presidential administration wanted to do away with civil rights regulations like Title IX of the Education Act (prohibiting discrimination in education) or Title VII of the 1964 Civil Rights Act (prohibiting discrimination in private employment). Most liberal and minority support for the ERA was based on such economic considerations.

There was also growing recognition that more and more women were running households by themselves with very little income. The trend was called "the feminization of poverty" and it covered women of all races. A report by the National Advisory Council on Economic Opportunity showed the number of female heads of households increased more than 30 percent between 1970 and 1979 to a total of 8,456,000, with one in every three households living in poverty (in comparison with one in eighteen, in male-headed households). Facts like these were taken in hand when ERA supporters lobbied legislators to approve ratification. Supporters believed that if representatives learned how difficult many women's lives were, they would vote for equal rights.

As with the opposition campaign, most women who worked for the ERA were not professional lobbyists or career activists. They were "extraordinary, ordinary citizens" as one volunteer put it, women who cared enough about the cause to donate days, nights, and weekends—whatever time they could afford. These were the women who went to the state capitols to buttonhole legislators and tell them why equal rights were important. Across the country they stuffed envelopes with ERA literature, made phone calls, handed out leaflets, organized meetings, rallies, and fund-raising events, marched in parades, and took care of the dozens of details that go into running a political campaign. While the national headquarters of organizations like NOW supervised the flow of resources to trouble spots, feeding their members information on the progress of the campaign, it was really up to volunteer workers at the local level to put steam behind the campaign.

ERA volunteers had two main objectives: to boost public support for the ERA everywhere, including ratified states where rescission was threatened, and to convince legislators in unratified states to vote for ratification. Volunteers usually came from a variety of organizations and worked together as a coalition. This was the case in Alaska, where a coalition worked to defeat a rescission threat. (The coalition's experience was similar to that of volunteers in many other states.)

In 1980, national officers of the Moral Majority went to Alaska to help promote a growing movement toward conservative, right-wing philosophy. Both Phyllis Schlafly and the Reverend Jerry Falwell flew to Anchorage to instruct and inspire a large audience in ways to defeat liberal ideas. One goal of the Alaskan Moral Majority was to get the state legislature to overturn its vote on the ERA. Schlafly formed chapters of the Eagle Forum, and instructed the members in lobbying and letter-writing techniques. While the press covered the visit and reported on several public meetings, the hidden agenda to overturn ratification was not generally known. ERA supporters, however, understood what was going on.

Moral Majority and Eagle Forum members started talking to legislators, trying to determine whether they had enough support to challenge the ERA and push a rescission bill at the next legislative session. While they did their head count, ERA volunteers mounted a very quiet but intense drive to identify supporters in case they had to prove to legislators that the majority of voters didn't want to rescind ratification. Identifying supporters was crucial, so that pro-ERA forces could move quickly and forcefully if a rescission vote popped up.

A political organizer from NOW in Washington, D.C., flew to Anchorage to teach "phone bank" techniques. Following her advice, a telephone "script" was prepared and business owners were asked to donate the use of their telephones. Volunteers would then go to these phones at nights and on the weekends and call a list of identified potential supporters, whose names had been given by pro-ERA organizations. The script told the callers exactly what to say. When a supporter was identified, he or she was asked a variety of questions. For instance, "Can we send a telegram to a representative in your name and bill it to you?" "How many messages are you willing to pay for?" "Can you share with us the names of other supporters you might know?"

Lining up support was "an invisible struggle," Anchorage organizer Joyce Mansfield Rivers said. "We chose not to advertise what we were doing. We were just getting ready so that we could move quickly if necessary." But as it happened, the opposition failed in their head count and decided not to press for rescission because they didn't have enough votes to win.

With the crisis over, ERA volunteers went back to fund-raising activities in order to send money to unratified states. Some Alaskans even traveled to other states to help in their campaigns. Oklahoma-born Dolly Krone, a senior in her late sixties, went four thousand miles from Anchorage to Tulsa, Oklahoma, "to do work that most people didn't realize was so important because it was drudgery." Krone worked seven days a week for twenty-six days, setting up a file system so that volunteers, supporters, and financial donors could be readily identified. Others in Oklahoma were tramping door to door in neighborhoods, shaking hands, and trying to win friends.

All this activity at the grass-roots level was largely unnoticed by the general public. This was because of a casual attitude about the ERA by the media. No newspaper or broadcasting station assigned a full-time reporter to the ERA because editors and news directors didn't think it was an important enough issue. There was coverage for the big events, but only women's magazines and a handful of individual newspaper writers kept on top of ERA news. Among the writers, one feminist became popular during the ERA movement: columnist Ellen Goodman of the *Boston Globe*. Many of Goodman's columns zeroed in on arguments sent forth by ERA opponents. Targeting the insurance industry, for example, Goodman reminded readers that blacks were once charged more for life insurance than whites, but the practice was stopped when it became socially unacceptable. And while Mormons and Seventh Day Adventists live longer than other people, they have never been placed in a separate risk category that would raise their rates, Goodman said. There is nothing sacred about risk classifications which determine how much a person pays for insurance; why should sex be the criteria for rate setting, she asked? Why should females pay more for life insurance and get back less on pension plans because women on the average live longer than men? Where you live, how you live, are factors that can also be considered.

"The all-too-chivalrous rebuttal from the insurance industry now is that women aren't really suffering under this two-track system. Indeed, they insist, equality will cost women dearly. But whenever someone protests that equality will hurt women, watch out," Goodman warned her readers.

As a journalist, Goodman had the courage to point an accusing finger at ERA opponents like the insurance industry. But another feminist, Sonia Johnson, got headlines without ever intending to be news. A Mormon homemaker and part-time teacher, Johnson stunned people with the extent of her commitment to the ERA.

In 1978, Johnson, who lived in suburban Washington, D.C., testified in the U.S. Senate in behalf of the ERA extension. Utah Senator Orrin Hatch, a Mormon lay priest, was infuriated by Johnson when she said he was wrong in claiming that 100 percent of the Mormon Church was against the ERA. "In our church, women don't talk back to men, and when I disagreed with him, he got so angry he lost control. By the end he was yelling at me that I thought I was superior to all those other good Mormon women. He even accused me of insulting his wife!" Johnson later told *Ms.* reporter Lisa Cronin Wohl.

The remarkable thing about Johnson was that she didn't sit down and shut up, even though that message was given to her in clear terms by church members. She continued working for the ERA after the ratification deadline was extended, making a point of telling the public how Mormons were being coached to work against the Amendment. She exposed what had been a church secret: how members were ordered to lobby, leaflet, and make contributions to anti-ERA campaigns. They were told to say their activities were voluntary and unorganized, she said. "They are directed to say that they are concerned citizens following the dictates of their individual consciences," she told one gathering. "Since they are in fact following the very direct dictates of the Prophet's conscience and would revise their own overnight if he were to revise his, nothing could be further from the truth." ("The Prophet" is the head of the Mormon church.)

But even while speaking in favor of the ERA, Johnson considered herself a good Mormon. By her estimate, some 20 percent of all Mormons favored the Amendment, and she saw no grave conflict between supporting the ERA and her Mormon life-style. She belonged to the women's Relief Society, played the organ in church, and kept a traditional Mormon home for her husband and four children. But because she not only supported the Amendment, but also exposed the church's efforts to kill it, Johnson was not to be tolerated. She alone was put on trial by the church fathers for being unworthy of church membership. The verdict in the secret proceedings was that she was guilty of rash statements harmful to the church. Johnson was excommunicated and banned from taking part in rituals and sacraments. Excommunication was the church's most severe punishment, and it applied to both this life and any life hereafter. Sonia Johnson was told she could never join her family in heaven.

Being punished by her church was very painful. But in spite of her personal losses, Johnson came out of the ordeal as a dedicated feminist. She used her experience to inspire other women to stand up for their beliefs. As a new women's leader, Johnson joined a handful of people who were known nationally for their work in behalf of ERA.

Liz Carpenter, a Texan, already had a reputation in politics when she went to work for the ERA. A former White House press secretary, Carpenter was co-chair of ERAmerica, a nonpartisan organization formed to encourage ratification. A plain-talking, good-natured, energetic leader, Carpenter traveled the country, urging support for the Amendment. Carpenter saw her work for ERA as the dues she owed other women for having had a good career and a fascinating life. She tried to get other professionals on the ERA bandwagon, and liked the self-mocking slogan "Uppity women unite!"

Carpenter was not the first feminist in her family. Her great-aunts had worked for women's suffrage fifty years before. But Carpenter said the ladylike tactics her aunts had used to promote suffrage weren't going to work in pressuring states for ratification of the

ERA. She hoped that ERAmerica's toughest strategy—getting organizations to boycott unratified states by refusing to give them convention business—would tip the scales in states with stubborn legislatures.

"Certainly we've tried everything on the last 15 states," Carpenter told Patricia Lasher, the author of *Texas Women*, in 1979. "In the middle of the night when I wrestle with what we're going to do, because we're so close and yet so far, a lot of things go through my mind. Conventions which are boycotting the states which haven't ratified are helping. New Orleans is losing many groups at the last minute to Houston. It is hard to get front-page coverage of feminist news, but when you talk about big money, in the millions, which is being lost to a city or state because of failure to ratify the ERA, you make the front page."

Getting noticed was one of the problems ERA supporters faced. In an effort to grab some of the spotlight from Phyllis Schlafly, ERAmerica and other pro-ERA groups decided to use celebrities to publicize the cause. One of these was Alan Alda, best known for his work on the television series M*A*S*H. Alda was co-chair of the ERA Committee for the National Commission on the Observance of International Women's Year. At rallies, on television, and in print interviews he talked about what was in ERA for men, as well as for women. He said men would find new freedom when men and women share equally and men no longer have to be macho. Alda said that as women fill traditional male roles as police chiefs, gas station attendants, baseball players, and bankers, men will come to realize that wisdom, aggressiveness, and physical courage are not theirs alone. "We can still be strong and brave, but we won't feel we're the only ones who are," he said in a *Ms.* magazine interview. He said men also have paid a price for the submissiveness of women. "The clinging vine can be a Venus's flytrap," he said.

Alda talked about legal changes that would benefit men. He described Social Security laws that deny certain benefits to husbands; prejudice against male parents who seek child custody; welfare regulations that force a jobless husband from his home so that his wife can collect Aid to Dependent Children payments; and unfair divorce and alimony stipulations that cripple men economically.

Along with Alda, other celebrities who got on the ERA bandwagon were Ossie Davis, Lorne Greene, Judy Collins, Linda Evans, Mary Tyler Moore, Tony Randall, Norman Lear, Marlo Thomas, and Linda Lavin, among others. But there was no single person in any sphere whose name meant ERA in the same sense that Phyllis Schlafly's name came to mean Stop-ERA. Instead, the National Organization for Women (NOW) became most closely identified with the cause, with whoever was serving as president being most visible in the campaign during her tenure in office. From 1977 to the ratification deadline, June 30, 1982, the president was Eleanor Smeal, a homemaker from Pittsburgh, Pennsylvania.

Smeal was the first homemaker to head NOW. In fact, it was her experience as a housebound wife and mother that led her to become a feminist. In 1969 she spent a year in bed with a back ailment. Her husband, Charles, a metallurgist, did many of the household tasks, but the Smeals had to hire a woman to come in and take care of their children while Charles was at work. Questions came up: How did the hired woman live on the modest pay she received for taking care of children and doing housework? How did most families manage when the wife and mother was ill? Why was there no disability insurance for homemakers? Smeal started reading women's history and looking for answers to her questions. When she recovered from her illness, both she and Charles joined NOW.

Smeal had some experience in politics before she got involved with NOW. The daughter of Italian immigrants, she grew up in a home where arguing politics was an evening's entertainment. As a student at Duke University in North Carolina, she worked for racial integration on campus, losing an election as dormitory president because of her principles. She graduated from Duke with high honors and planned to study law, but when she learned that women seldom got to try cases in the courtroom, she settled for further studies in political science and public administration instead. Later, as a Pennsylvania homemaker, she worked with the League of Women Voters and served on the Allegheny County Council. It was when she discovered NOW that her interests were keenly focused and she began what was to become a full-time career as an activist.

Within seven years—working on the local, state, then national levels—Smeal became president of NOW. Her top priorities were getting homemakers into the organization, and getting ERA ratified. Smeal often testified before congressional committees, providing representatives with data on women's issues. She wanted Congress to understand the economics of the ERA, but she was just as determined that housewives should understand it. In her opinion, it was vital to their well-being.

A homemaker deserves economic security from a marriage partnership, she told *McCall's* magazine writer Martha Hewson. "Just because one person's name is on the paycheck does not mean that the other person isn't working. They made an agreement. One person is working for pay and the other person is working to take care of the kids and house. Basically they both are working. The legal fiction that it's his money and not hers, should be ended. I think it's their money!"

"Ellie" Smeal was tough, but soft-spoken and effective as a leader. As she wished, she appealed to a new group of women while in office and realized one of her goals. NOW membership doubled and became—at one hundred thousand—the largest feminist organization in the world. Many of the new members contributed to the ERA campaign. Letter writing, marching and fund-raising were by and large carried out by local chapters of NOW working with other women's organizations such as the National Federation of Business and Professional Women and the American Association of University Women.

While it was her own independent study of women's history that led Eleanor Smeal to champion equal rights, many younger women became interested because of new course work being offered. In the 1970s, universities offered a thousand women's studies courses that ranged from "Sexism in Schools" to "Women in Spanish Culture." Young leaders like Deborah DeBare became committed to equal rights after being introduced to women's history and realizing it was possible to alter history now. DeBare took a leave of absence from Brown University after her sophomore year to organize ERA volunteers on dozens of college campuses. She persuaded student volunteers to give up their vacations to work in unratified states. Following her lead, some thirty students agreed not only to sacrifice vacations, but also to take a semester off to work for the ERA.

A disturbing issue for young women in connection with the ERA was the possibility of being drafted into military service. In the late 1970s when Congress was considering reopening the draft to build a stronger military force, there was much debate about women taking equal responsibility with men to serve in the armed forces. (When Congress ordered registration for the draft in 1980, it didn't include women.) If the ERA were passed, draft registration would have to include women. Young women searched their minds and hearts for a fair answer to the dilemma. While some wanted to serve, others felt they should not serve in the military as long as there was inequality in other phases of life. But what if the ERA passed and females were declared equal under the law?

Julie Melrose, a draft-age feminist, described the mixed feelings young women had to sort through to arrive at a position on the draft. She wrote a letter to the editor at *Ms.*:

> I'm grieved that one result of a 10-year struggle to improve the quality of women's lives may be the increased participation of women in the military, but I understand that it's part of a process and that we will inevitably open some doors through which many of us prefer not to walk. Every time a traditionally male stronghold—no matter how unsavory—is forced to admit women, we do become a little freer.

Like Julie Melrose, other young people kept hoping for a "freer" future right up to the ratification deadline. In Syracuse, New York, Michele Michael organized ERA support at her high school graduation in June 1982. Graduating seniors carried "ERA Yes" balloons on stage with them to receive their diplomas and awards. For supporters young and old, passage of the ERA was no more than a matter of "simple justice"—a phrase heard often in the long campaign. At stake was the possibility of women becoming full partners. in the American system for the first time.

The passion women felt for equal rights was shown in Houston at the beginning of the 1977 IWY conference. Two thousand female runners had carried a torch in relays from Seneca Falls, New York, where the first women's rights conference was held. The arrival of the torch was described in an official report on the conference, *The Spirit of Houston*:

> For the dramatic last mile, three young Houston athletes ran together, accompanied by scores of delegates. A shout went up when the waiting crowd spotted the bronze torch being held aloft by the pale arm of Peggy Kokernot, marathon runner; the golden arm of Sylvia Ortiz, a senior at the University of Houston; and the dark-skinned arm of 16-year-old high school track star Michele Cearcy. "ERA! ERA! ERA!" the crowd chanted. "Hey, Hey, What Do You Say? Ratify the ERA! ERAERAERAERA."

THE FINAL
CAMPAIGN
AND HOW IT
FAILED

The "simple justice" that supporters hoped for from the ERA was not to be realized by 1982. This fact became a grim possibility about halfway down the road to the final deadline. Early ratification of the Amendment by a majority of the states had been misleading. It was as though the ERA bandwagon had rolled merrily along and then had come smack against a brick wall.

When the Twenty-seventh Amendment was first approved by Congress in 1972, there was a climate of enthusiasm for women's rights. ERA supporters believed their cause was righteous, so there was no reason why it would fail. By the end of 1973, thirty state legislatures ratified the Amendment, scarcely pausing for debate; three more states followed suit in 1974. But only one state was added in 1975; there were no ratifications in 1976; and Indiana accepted the ERA by a margin of a single legislator's vote in 1977. That was the last nod of approval, bringing the tally to thirty-five states. Thirty-eight were needed.

A focused campaign to win ratification began in 1976. That year, major organizations supporting the ERA decided that nationally coordinated efforts had to be directed at trouble spots in specific states or the ERA movement would fail. ERAmerica, a professionally run, bipartisan political campaign organization was conceived by NOW, Common Cause, the National Federation of Business and

Professional Women's Clubs, LWV, AAUW, and several church and labor groups. Nineteen seventy-seven was targeted as the year to boost ERA over the top.

For the women's movement, 1977 could be remembered as both the best of years and the worst of years. The big plus was the success of the International Women's Year conference in Houston, which created a sense of mutual commitment never reached on such a scale before. Many women left Houston feeling renewed and ready for whatever struggles awaited them; their enthusiasm spread itself beyond the boundaries of that southern city. But at the same time, each motion passed at the Houston meeting had been an alarm signal to the anti-feminist/anti-ERA opposition. What they were experiencing was a personal attack on their values, with one issue after another adding up to a horrible assault. One fundamentalist preacher railed against the "moral rottenness" of the agenda. He said it meant the killing of unborn children, lesbianism, and the destruction of home and family through the ERA.

Lesbianism was seen as the logical result of feminist ideology. If men are oppressors, women liberationists will neither honor them nor live with them, it was said. Clay Smothers, a black Texas state representative at the IWY meeting, expressed the homophobia felt by many. "I have enough civil rights to choke a hungry goat. I ask for public rights . . . victory over perverts of this country. I want a right to segregate my family from these misfits and perverts." From the time of the Houston conference, ERA became synonymous with gay rights in many people's minds.

ERA opponents also began to pick up on some feminist attitudes that were insulting to homemakers and nonprofessional laborers. Being "just a housewife" was something to be ashamed of, feminist rhetoric suggested. Gloria Steinem, one of the most sensitive and egalitarian leaders in the women's movement, risked being misunderstood when she told audiences that "women's work is----work." In another instance, a writer calculated in a national magazine article that a housewife, if properly paid for her services, would earn seven hundred dollars a week. "Don't you think a woman should be paid more than a common bus driver?" the article asked. Bus drivers and other blue-collar workers had reason to resent such elitist remarks.

In this atmosphere of values in conflict, anti-ERA forces got stronger. Stopping ERA became one of the priorities in right-wing legislative politics. In the Nevada legislature, where Mormons held the reins of the most powerful committees, a group of legislators who had promised to support the ERA reversed their votes at the last minute and let it go down to defeat. It was impossible to prove what deals had been made in political horse trading—who promised what in exchange for their votes against the ERA—but the shifts in position could not otherwise be explained. ERA backers in Nevada were bitterly disappointed. But nationwide, prospects for ratification were believed by ERAmerica to be best in several other states: Illinois, Florida, North Carolina, and Virginia. If ratification was not approved in one session of a state legislature, the plan was to press for a positive vote in the next. (An issue can surface repeatedly in a legislative body; it is not necessarily dead if it fails during one particular session.)

Illinois had a unique law requiring not a simple majority but a three-fifths vote of the legislature to ratify a constitutional amendment. ERA supporters discovered that more than a quarter of the Illinois legislators had strong ties with the insurance industry, and that these representatives voted consistently against the ERA. But revealing these connections didn't do much to upset the legislature's conscience. Each time ratification was the question, it was turned down. In 1977 it lost in Illinois by six votes.

The measure fared no better in other targeted states. In Florida and North Carolina, it was two votes shy of passage in 1977. And in Virginia, just one vote. NOW's leader, Eleanor Smeal, said, "We need a national campaign of increasing outrage. We need to recruit people to go to all the states, create caravans to go into every small hamlet and build a grass-roots organization. . . . We need national boycotts, economic sanctions. We have to make this too hot an issue to trade on." But only in Indiana was the measure successful in 1977. But in Indiana victory was blighted by Phyllis Schlafly's claim that it was only due to First Lady Rosalyn Carter's "southern charm" and her promises to campaign for a state senator if he voted for the ERA.

As promised, a national boycott was organized in that year of intense activity and painful defeat. Miami, New Orleans, and Las Vegas were blacklisted as convention sites by organizations sympathetic to the ERA. At the same time, the National Women's Political Caucus (NWPC), the political wing of the women's rights movement, started raising money and working to defeat anti-ERA legislators. (The name for their campaign, Throw the Rascals Out.) NOW also created internships to train women to work for passage of the measure. "ERA missionaries" coordinated by NOW and ER-America went from their home states to targeted states to assist in canvassing door to door and identifying ERA supporters. From the nation's capital, President Jimmy Carter sent Vice-President Walter Mondale and various aides to the states to persuade local legislators.

Pressure from the White House was especially aggravating to the leader of the opposition. Biographer Carol Felsenthal wrote, "For every one Washington lobbyist dispatched to the provinces by Jimmy Carter, Phyllis Schlafly dispatched a hundred Stop-ERAers—housewives from the legislator's own district who could make or break him in the next election." Speaking into a bullhorn at rallies, Schlafly told her troops that Carter was blackmailing legislators by threatening to withhold funds for state and local projects.

Time and again, Schlafly shifted attention from the status of women to the status of government. Her theme: If you pass ERA the Washington bureaucracy will be on your backs. "The real beneficiaries of the ERA are the federal politicians and payrollers because they see it as an enormous transfer of power from the states to the federal government. People won't stand for that anymore. The whole momentum of the country is moving away from that."

Whether state legislators feared big government, worried about being voted out of office if they supported ERA, or whether they were indifferent to the measure, it was clear by 1978 that the three state legislatures still needed would not ratify by the 1979 deadline. On top of that, strong Stop-ERA lobbying had also led five states—Tennessee, Kentucky, Idaho, Nebraska, and South Dakota—to rescind their ratification votes on the grounds that lawmakers had acted too fast when they approved it. With these obstacles, supporters of the Amendment called for an extension of the ratification deadline, as well as a Supreme Court ruling on the rescissions.

ERA campaign leaders reasoned that the prospect of three more years of fighting over the measure would convince legislators they might as well vote for it and get rid of the whole disagreeable situation, so they lobbied Congress hard to get the necessary extension. They also felt that a court ruling allowing states to rescind ratification would be overturned. It was a relief when Congress settled both issues in favor of the ERA. Congress voted by a simple majority to grant an extension with a new deadline of June 30, 1982, and also voted against allowing the states to change their previous ratification positions.

Not surprisingly, Schlafly jumped on the extension. She said decisions on constitutional questions should be made by a two-thirds vote of Congress; a simple majority decision was itself unconstitutional. A number of major newspapers agreed with her, as did some proponents of the ERA. (Congress had considered the two-thirds plan, but rejected it. As it was, the vote on allowing the extension fell just short of a two-thirds majority.) But in spite of the extension, Stop-ERA held a victory banquet in Washington in March 1979 celebrating the sure death of the measure. Schlafly was the centerpiece of the banquet and she told an audience of fifteen hundred women in gowns and corsages they had given "the bureaucrats and politicians" a stunning defeat.

Schlafly was confident the extension would do the ERA no good, but she continued to orchestrate the efforts that made her coalition effective and highly visible. In North Carolina in 1979 two thousand women created a prayer chain at the state capitol, asking God to once and for all defeat "this thing." In Florida and Nevada, general election ballots asked voters for their preference on ratification (as a guide for legislators). In both states, the majority of people who went to the polls said, "Don't ratify." In Florida, when both the governor and aides of President Carter tried to persuade key senators to change their votes, Stop-ERA workers sent Elmer's Glue to anti-ERA lawmakers urging them to "stay glued to your seat." In Illinois, there were charges that the governor was merely using a pro-ERA position to further his career. Also in Illinois, bad publicity was created for the ERA cause when a NOW organizer was indicted by a grand jury for allegedly offering one thousand dollars for a "Yes" vote.

While these incidents were coloring the ERA drama, larger economic and social changes were also taking place that may have helped stall the ratification process.

In the early 1970s when the Amendment was first ratified by more than thirty states, the economic condition of the country was strong. There were plenty of jobs, business was good, and no one felt especially threatened by women getting better opportunities and higher pay. Within the decade, however, the cycle shifted. Unemployment was an increasing problem by the late 1970s, and businesses were looking for ways to cut back, not to share the wealth. In this atmosphere, women's demands for more money and upward mobility were no longer so welcome.

Politically, those who may have been indifferent to women's rights were alarmed at the idea of federal interference at the state and local levels. Just as federal judges had ordered forced integration of the Boston school system through busing—a decision that led to violence and seemingly endless racial hostility—so Schlafly raised a vision of equally disturbing intervention in local practices. Many conservatives worried that their lives would be altered by federal judges, whom they did not elect and could not control. Schlafly said that not only federal judges but Congress would be taking over states' rights. She kept Section Two of the Amendment in the public eye ("The Congress shall have the power to enforce, by appropriate legislation, the provisions of this article"), painting a picture of relentless federal interference everywhere from the school to marital relationships.

Two inflammatory issues that hurt the ERA were abortion and the draft. When in 1973 the Supreme Court legalized the use of abortion procedures in the first three months of pregnancy, advocates believed that a major sanction against women's rights had been lifted. Unwanted pregnancies, clandestine and dangerous procedures, were assumed to be a closed chapter in women's history. (Before the Supreme Court decision, which was based on a woman's constitutional right to privacy, the separate states controlled the legality of abortion procedures.) But objections to the court's decision had not been reckoned with. On the sixth anniversary of the ruling, demonstrations and counterdemonstrations came to a head. Nearly sixty thousand abortion opponents marched on the White House carrying red roses "as a beautiful living reminder of the preborn child."

That same day at the National Abortion Rights Action League, feminist leader Gloria Steinem held up a picture of another "rose." Rosaura Jimenez, a twenty-seven-year-old woman, had died of an illegal abortion following Congress's 1979 restriction on the use of Medicaid monies for most abortion procedures. "This is true human cost," Steinem asserted. "The point now is not one of conscience or morality but of choice. The other side has the right not to have an abortion but what's going on now is a struggle for political control." As it happened, control was shifting more and more to political conservatives. In 1981 Congress voted even more limits on federal funds for abortion. Talk about a constitutional amendment to prohibit even the choice of abortion was heard increasingly, along with growing resistance to the ERA.

People from all political persuasions were alarmed when the draft issue came up in 1980. Because of an emergency situation in the Middle East (the Soviet Union had invaded Afghanistan, and Iran was holding American Embassy personnel hostage), the need for a strong military force seemed imminent. President Carter called for draft registration of nineteen- and twenty-year-old men and women. All four military service chiefs recommended registering women, but the public outcry was overwhelming. A scene in Senator Nancy Kassebaum's office showed how alarmed some people were at the idea of drafting women. Eight Pentecostal ministers told the Senator it was scripturally sound to reinstitute draft registration for men, citing chapter and verse of the Bible which, they believed prophesied a Soviet take-over of the Middle East. But to include women was anti-God and anti-family, they declared, and would do no less than rot the moral fiber of America.

The ministers need not have feared. It was not the time for social initiatives in Congress. After listening to a great deal of testimony pro and con on the issue, Congress voted for an all-male registration. A subsequent appeal to the Supreme Court found the Court maintaining Congress's position on grounds that the courts must defer to lawmakers in national security matters. One result of this decision was that in Virginia, legislators voted against the ERA on the grounds that if the Amendment passed, women would have to go to the trenches. It was true that if the ERA were ratified neither Congress nor the courts could likely stop female registration, but registration was no guarantee of being drafted, least of all of being drafted into combat service.

Other setbacks that helped put ratification in doubt included a variety of legal opinions such as another Supreme Court decision saying divorced persons are not entitled to share their former spouse's military pension. Women also lost cases challenging veterans' preference in government hiring; and judges started denying discrimination claims unless it was established that women were victims of *intentional* discrimination—which is difficult to prove. In other downtrends, Iowa rejected a state ERA, while in Congress some members worked to get rid of affirmative action programs that require minorities and women to be hired for government-funded jobs and admitted to educational programs. Affirmative action opponents claimed that quotas discriminated against white males. President Ronald Reagan's administration cut federal budgets for Social Security and welfare programs, both of which were badly needed by poor people, especially poor women.

So while arguments against the ERA were increasing, the need for it grew. In 1981 NOW identified six unratified states where efforts would be concentrated. Several had turned down the ERA in past legislative sessions, but there was always hope to change public opinion and thereby change the legislators' votes. Florida, Illinois, Oklahoma, North Carolina, Virginia, and Missouri were targeted for door-to-door leafletting, public information campaigns, and legislative lobbying. The state of Virginia, however, fell with the draft issue, and in Missouri a bill calling for ratification was killed in legislative committee.

Answering NOW's call, women in ratified states raised money to send ERA volunteers to the four crucial states. There was deep concern that the Amendment would fail. Attorney Dorothy Ames Haaland, a NOW fund raiser in Alaska, expressed a common frustration. "We're not getting to the people who need it most—the homemakers and a lot of women active in church groups. They are being frightened and told it's not Christian. We have to reach out and get them interested. There must be some way to make contact and open minds," Haaland said.

Getting correct information to the public about the Amendment was clearly a problem. An Oklahoma newspaper poll showed an interesting discrepancy that proved this. When asked how they felt about the ERA, Oklahomans approved of it by a narrow majority. But when they were shown the actual wording of the measure—which seemed to be substantially different from what they *thought* it was—over 80 percent of the population approved it. But not so the representatives. In the Oklahoma legislature Senator Norman Lamb said, "I hope and pray that women, ladies, and girls will not be dragged down to the level of men by the passage of the 27th Amendment." The measure failed in the Oklahoma Senate by a vote of twenty-seven to twenty-one. ERA supporters unfurled a yellow banner for the lawmakers to read: *Equality Denied 1982*.

Florida was the same old story. The Senate defeated ratification by a vote of twenty-two to sixteen. "Vote them out!" and "We'll remember in November!" ERA workers shouted. Eleanor Smeal said, "We started this campaign thinking we were coming to bodies of debate and wisdom. . . . Well, we know better now. We are never again going to beg men for our rights!"

In North Carolina, 60 percent of the citizens supported the Amendment while 31 percent were against it. Yet a group of state senators went to the legislators' chapel where they took a "solemn pledge" to kill the ERA. The Amendment was tabled, in spite of the people's approval. Again the cry "Vote them out!" and again the committee system had shown how a measure can be bottlenecked when a powerful legislator or a small group of legislators hold a piece of legislation at the committee stage and keep it from reaching the floor for a vote.

In Illinois, one of the most powerful representatives was Senate Speaker George Ryan. It was observed that each time a senator tried to discuss a plan to do away with the three-fifths rule for ratification and instead require only a simple majority to ratify (any number over 50 percent) as other states did, Ryan ruled him out of order and closed the meeting. The question of majority rule versus the three-fifths rule in Illinois, therefore, became the focus of the pro-ERA campaign. There were more than enough votes for ratification if the majority ruled.

A huge campaign was launched to persuade the Speaker, the governor, and the legislators that the rule should be allowed to come to the floor for a vote by the members. Tactics included television advertisements with Chicago Mayor Jane Byrne and Illinois resident Marlo Thomas. There were "Help Pass ERA" spots with Alan Alda, Paul Newman, Lauren Bacall, Carol Burnett, Esther Rolle, and others. Signature ads in the newspapers were signed by state and national organizations, and big names like Betty and Gerald Ford, Jimmy and Rosalyn Carter, U.S. senators and representatives. Constitutional lawyers and professional lobbyists pitched ERA information at legislators. There was a blitz of brochures, meetings, door-to-door canvassing, vigils, and picket lines.

When it was clear that the Illinois political machinery could not be dynamited loose, deeply committed supporters turned in despair to fasting and civil disobedience. Twenty women chained themselves to the brass railing outside the Senate chambers in Springfield to "dramatize the economic slavery we are in." On May 18, 1982, seven women went on a hunger strike. They sat in the capitol rotunda each day reminding spectators, whether they liked it or not, of their profound attachment to the principle of equal rights. Sonia Johnson, the excommunicated Mormon, was among the strikers. Her weight fell from 122 pounds to 104 and she had to be hospitalized for illness.

Stop-ERA volunteers ate candy bars in front of the fasting women. They printed bumper stickers that said: *They need to lose weight anyway.* One pro-ERA senator was annoyed at the unladylike conduct of the fasters. He called it "political extortion" and said he would withhold his support until the women stopped it.

There was no rules change. In the Illinois Senate on June 22, the vote was thirty-one for and twenty-seven against ratification. Angry feminists dropped plastic bags filled with animal blood outside the capitol and scrawled the names of prominent ERA opponents in the blood. Nine women were arrested and led away in handcuffs. Governor James Thompson, whose lukewarm support had angered ERA proponents, called the blood smearing "vile and disgusting." He said it was the same as "painting swastikas on synagogues." In the Illinois House, the vote was 103 for and 72 against. All in all, ratification had fallen nine votes short of passage. The House vote ended the women's thirty-seven-day hunger strike.

Just before the final, fateful votes were cast in the various states in June, ERA supporters across the country had converged on state capitals in Florida, Illinois, Oklahoma, and North Carolina. Chicago Mayor Jane Byrne, North Carolina Governor Jim Hunt, NOW ERA Countdown Chair Betty Ford, and NOW President Ellie Smeal joined scores of volunteers marching to the legislatures wearing the colors of the historic suffrage campaign. Men and women in white, carrying white, purple, and gold banners, proclaimed one more time their desire for equal rights in the Constitution. A network of supporters interlocked across the country.

From Bismarck, North Dakota, they went to Springfield, Illinois. From New York, they went to Florida. Alaskans went to Raleigh, North Carolina. Oregonians went to Oklahoma City. The week after the final marches and rallies, *Time* magazine carried a half-page story on ERA activities in Illinois, where details were especially vivid. The cover story of the nation's top news magazine, however, was about a heavyweight boxer and a "macho" movie star. Even in its final hours, the ERA was seldom front page news.

In the end, the only thing that counts in politics is the vote, and the ERA didn't get it. *Time* ran its postmortem, "What Killed Equal Rights?" in early July, with pictures of Smeal and Schlafly. The captions read, "Eleanor Smeal: blunt, tenacious, but inept in the world of politics" and "Phyllis Schlafly: adroit, determined, playing to people's worst fears."

Smeal had actually conceded defeat at a June 24 rally that officially ended the ERA Countdown Campaign. She told a crowd of two thousand in Washington, D.C., "We are ending this campaign stronger than we began. We are a majority. We are determined to play majority politics.... We are not going to be reduced again to the ladies' auxiliary."

Smeal named specific situations that had to be addressed before ratification could be achieved in the future. She faulted both political parties. The Republican Party had dropped the ERA from its platform and deserted women's rights; 83 percent of all registered Republicans lived in unratified states. The Democratic Party had given lip service to the issue, but had failed to make it a high priority and to put money and human resources behind it.

She went on to cite special corporate interests that profit from sex discrimination. "On the list of organizations that support the ERA, which includes hundreds of organizations from nearly every walk of life, major business interests are notable by their absence. There are no Chambers of Commerce, no Associations of Manufacturers, no Insurance Councils," Smeal said. There were, however, the names of many corporate interests on the list of contributors to Mountain States Legal Foundation, an organization which opposed the deadline extension and led a court fight against it.

Finally, the NOW leader pointed to the sex bias in state legislatures. "Men are 94 percent of all state senators and 86 percent of all state representatives." It had already been seen that legislatures were reflecting an upsurge of rigid political and religious conservatism in the country. They were following President Reagan's lead in dropping civil rights commitments and opposing legally mandated opportunities for women and minorities. Local NOW groups were asked to start working to vote out of office lawmakers who represented such trends. At the end of the ERA drive, the National Women's Political Caucus issued a "dirty dozen" hit list of state legislators, all male, who blocked ratification. They also pledged to elect women to office in far greater numbers.

In reviewing the long campaign, it was seen that pro-ERA activity had often been spontaneous and self-directed. This had led to confusion and little systematic coordination of efforts. Many times people looking for information on the Amendment were unable to find sources. All too often, people who said they supported the measure did not know exactly what it was. They believed it was an equal pay provision. They did not know that it applied to federal and state governments. Or they did not know the difference between state ERAs and the federal measure. Furthermore, those who *did* know the ABCs of the Amendment did not seize opportunities to discuss the second clause (granting Congress the right to enforce the law). This gave Schlafly the upper hand and a chance to hammer away at her case on federal interference, without fear of contradiction.

A big mistake supporters made was in assuming that being right was enough. Righteousness seldom wins in legislative politics. Bill Harrington, an ERA field organizer, said that "educating" legislators was a very limited approach. "Only about one-third of a legislature really believes in an issue like the ERA. The others are political votes, and you have to go after them politically." Harrington said advice telling grass-roots lobbyists to be "quiet and professional" was also off base. "It's okay to be pushy. The politicians may not like it, but that's the language they respect."

Proponents also needed to put more pressure on identified supporters who didn't stand by their commitments. While organized labor officially endorsed the ERA, it used little of its influence to sway state legislators or the electorate. Organizations that vowed support, such as the American Home Economics Association and the American Psychiatric Association, nevertheless held conventions in boycotted cities—even against the objections of many of their members. And while an organization called the Religious Committee for the Equal Rights Amendment attracted nineteen member groups from different faiths, observers noted that equal rights for women was not as important to religious activists as equal rights for racial minorities had been in the 1960s. Even Episcopalians—who had agreed to ordain women as priests—did not have ERA on the agenda of a major churchwomen's convention.

So on one side, while there was a lot of support for ratification, it was widespread and often diffuse. On the other side there was more coherence with a mass organization revolving around a single, charismatic leader. In Phyllis Schlafly's camp there was no discussion, debate, show of hands, or weary efforts to arrive at a unified philosophy. Schlafly was in charge and everyone accepted her leadership. She had been training women in politics since 1968, and they were ready and willing to follow her lead when she called the shots. Beyond that, local organizations were free to run themselves as they wished. What they invariably wished was to please Phyllis.

The *National Review* ran an editorial entitled "Good Show, Phyllis" at the end of the ERA battle:

> Let it be said at once that Phyllis Schlafly is one of the most remarkable women in American history. It will not be said as often as it should be; certainly not in the ideologically engineered textbooks, full of "positive" images of women, that will be used in the NEA-dominated schools. She has triumphed over the major media, the bureaucrats (and bureaucrettes), and the "women's movement," almost single-handedly. ERA is dead.

Schlafly echoed the claim that ERA "is dead now and forever in this century." But supporters said, "No, the demand for equal rights is never going away."

At a Los Angeles rally on June 30, thousands of supporters including many young men and women drew together at midnight for a moment of symbolic darkness when the ERA "died." Then thousands of candles were lit to signify renewed commitment to the Amendment. The message in Los Angeles and across the nation from ERA supporters to any who doubted: *The dream will never die.*

The passion for equality would not fade.

EPILOGUE

On January 3, 1983, the Equal Rights Amendment was reintroduced in the House of Representatives. There were 230 co-sponsors; 290 votes were needed to pass it.

ERA supporters felt somewhat optimistic, although leaders of NOW and the National Women's Political Caucus had wanted to wait for the best possible timing. Still, 1982 elections had produced more pro-ERA legislators and women were gaining more political skills to lobby for ratification. NOW started an ERA Victory Fund, believing it could take one year, two years, or more to get the ERA into the Constitution.

There were five days of hearings on ERA II between July and November 1983. Testimony telling how the ERA would work was well presented, showing how effective six identical state ERAs had been. Testimony emphasized the difference the ERA makes in the economic lives of women. November 7, the House Judiciary Subcommittee approved the bill by a vote of six to two, with no amendments. November 9, the full Judiciary Committee passed the bill by a vote of twenty-one to ten, again defeating amendments that would outlaw abortion and a female draft. According to Representative Patricia Schroeder, "The debate was bitter and emotional."

NOW's new president, Judy Goldsmith, had a letter ready to mail to the membership. She anticipated no trouble getting ERA passed in the House. An enormous problem was expected in the Senate, now dominated by "New Right" Republicans Jesse Helms, Orrin Hatch, Strom Thurmond, and John East. Goldsmith called for a massive membership drive and fund-raising campaign to help elect sympathetic representatives in 1984 elections and "to make certain we have the human and financial resources needed to carry the ERA to victory this time, quickly and decisively." But before the letter could go into the mail at Thanksgiving, ERA II went down on the floor of the House.

The final vote was 278 for the Amendment, 147 against—six votes shy of the two-thirds quorum necessary for passage. According to the *Women's Political Times*, "Some blamed it on the Speaker of the House, some on the anti-choice lobby. Democrats pointed fingers at Republicans, Republicans at Democrats. . . . accusations ricocheted across the country."

What was known was that two days before the House vote, an anti-abortion group had lobbied intensely against the ERA, again linking it with abortion. Then, on the day of the vote, House Speaker Thomas P. (Tip) O'Neill, a Democrat, brought ERA to the floor under a "suspension of rules," which prohibits amendments and limits debate to forty minutes. This unusual move infuriated many of the Republican opposition, who said O'Neill had no right to suspend the rules on such an important issue, and that he was using the ERA just to make himself and his party look good. Said New York Representative Hamilton Fish, "A 'No' vote is not a vote against ERA, but a vote for respect for the U.S. Constitution."

Some representatives who voted against the Amendment claimed they would have voted for it, had there been an anti-abortion amendment tagged on. In any event, at a postvote conference women's leaders vowed to make the ERA a potent issue in future elections. "We now know the truth about our representatives' commitment to equality," NWPC Chair Kathy Wilson said, "and those who voted against us will soon learn the consequences."

FOR FURTHER
READING

The Equal Rights Handbook, by Riane Tennenhaus Eisler (New York: Avon Books, 1978), sets forth "facts and fancies" related to the ERA. Strategies for passing the Amendment compose about half the book.

A must for those interested in women's history is Betty Friedan's *The Feminine Mystique* (New York: Dell Publishing Co., 1963). This book was a catalyst for the present women's movement. For a broader view of women, see *A History of Women in America* by Carol Hymowitz and Michaele Weissman (New York: Bantam Books, 1978). This easy-to-read volume begins with the Revolutionary War and goes up to the new feminism.

For an understanding of Phyllis Schlafly in her own words, read *The Power of the Positive Woman* (Jove Publications, 1978). A biography of Phyllis Schlafly is Carol Felsenthal's *The Sweetheart of the Silent Majority* (Garden City, NY: Doubleday & Company, 1981).

Sisterhood Is Powerful (New York: Vintage Books, 1970), edited by Robin Morgan, is an anthology of writing from the women's movement. It provides further understanding of sexism, repression, and protest.

All of the documents and most of the testimony from the 1970 congressional hearings on the ERA can be found in *Women and the Equal Rights Amendment* (New York: Bowker, 1973), edited by Catharine R. Stimpson.

Most thought and opinion on the ERA has been published in periodicals, rather than books. Among these, *Ms.* magazine has provided the most consistent coverage from a supportive point of view. *The Phyllis Schlafly Report* and various magazines offer the opposing point of view. See *Reader's Guide to Periodical Literature* for magazine articles.

INDEX

24 COLLIER HEIGHTS

DATE DUE

24 COLLIER HEIGHTS